# One Man's Terrorist?

## *Violence, Labels, and the Politics of Fear*

How 'Terrorist' Became the
Most Dangerous Word in Politics

# Sean Hogan

# Dedication

*To those who have spoken out when silence was easier.*

*To the whistleblowers, the journalists, the mothers, the prisoners, the children, the truth-tellers, known and unknown, who risked everything for dignity and justice.*

*And to the memory of those labelled terrorist for simply daring to resist.*

*You are not forgotten.*

# Acknowledgement

This book could not have come into being without the support, courage and insight of many people.

To my family, who endured long nights and early mornings and gave me the space to write honestly, thank you for your patience and love.

To the colleagues, legal minds, researchers and quiet helpers who contributed sources, clarified law or challenged assumptions, your contributions sharpened the argument and deepened the truth.

To the countless journalists, human rights advocates and political prisoners whose stories inspired this work, you shaped more of these pages than you know.

To the readers willing to question everything, even themselves, this was written with you in mind.

Finally, to those in power, may you read this too and recognise that history always renders its own verdict.

# About the Author

Seán Hogan is a seasoned board leader, strategist, and social scientist whose career has spanned governance, public service, and complex negotiations across Ireland and the UK. A Chartered Director with decades of experience navigating political systems, regulatory environments, and high-stakes decision-making, he brings to his writing a rare blend of analytical discipline and lived insight into how power actually functions.

His lifelong interest in geopolitics, colonial legacies, and global justice has shaped a body of work that confronts difficult truths with clarity and compassion. Drawing on a background steeped in Ireland's own history of dispossession and political struggle, Hogan offers a distinctive perspective on the modern Middle East and the collapse of long-held narratives about Zionism, democracy, and Western influence.

*The Rise and Fall of Zionism in the 21st Century* is his most ambitious project to date, a sweeping, human-focused examination of ideology, morality, and the unraveling of a geopolitical myth.

# Preface

# Prologue:
# The Word That Ends Debate

"Terrorist." The word that ends debate. That shuts down conversation. That extinguishes nuance. Once applied, there is no trial, no defence, no context, only condemnation. It carries the weight of ultimate judgment, and when used, it leaves no space for complexity or contradiction. The word, once spoken, invokes immediate fear, disgust and moral clarity. And yet, for all its power and pervasiveness, it is a term without a universally accepted definition.

The power of the word *terrorist* lies not in what it describes, but in what it does. It delegitimises opposition. It justifies state violence. It sanctifies the narrative of those who wield it. When a state labels a person or a group as *terrorist*, that label often precedes evidence and outlives justice. There is no statute of limitations on being labelled a terrorist. There is no path to redemption. The label becomes the identity. This transformation is not incidental. It is central to the political utility of the word.

This book is not an attempt to excuse violence. It is an attempt to understand power, how language, more than bombs or bullets, is used to control perception. To control truth. To control morality itself.

## PART II: A Term Without Agreement

Despite being one of the most commonly used words in global politics, *terrorism* remains without a single, globally agreed definition. The United Nations has never settled on a standard. Governments construct contradictory lists of terrorist organisations. Legal systems bend the term to suit their needs. Journalists apply it inconsistently. Social media weaponises it.

The absence of agreement is not accidental. It is useful. Ambiguity permits flexibility. A vague term can be stretched to fit an evolving narrative. It can be tailored to protect allies and condemn enemies. It can be wrapped in legal language or shouted across a news chyron. Its elasticity is its strength and its danger.

In the name of counterterrorism, states have suspended civil liberties, launched wars, surveilled populations and silenced dissent. Yet the very definition of the threat they claim to be fighting remains elusive.

## PART III: The Narrative Weapon

A drone strike that kills a wedding party is called collateral damage. A homemade bomb that kills soldiers on patrol is called terrorism. A missile launched by the state is self-defence. A rock thrown by the stateless is violence. The act is the same: harm inflicted on a human life. But the judgment differs, because the authority to define has always belonged to the powerful.

Consider the case of the 1890 Wounded Knee Massacre, in which US cavalry troops killed hundreds of Lakota Sioux, including women and children. The soldiers responsible were awarded Medals of Honor, the nation's highest military decoration. In 2025, US Secretary of Defence Pete Hegseth affirmed that those medals would not be revoked. They were deserved, he said. A review panel had agreed. No matter that it was one of the bloodiest massacres in US history on American soil, and no matter that it was largely committed against unarmed people. The state had spoken, and the act was framed not as terrorism, not even as an atrocity, but as service. Honourable. Decorated.

Now reverse the scenario. Imagine the same massacre carried out not by uniformed soldiers under the American flag, but by an Indigenous resistance group seeking to reclaim occupied land. Would those men be remembered as heroes, or hunted as terrorists?

**PART IV: Narrator over Nature**

This is the core of the problem: violence is not named according to its effects, it is named according to its author. In that naming, entire political struggles are won or lost. Language becomes the weapon. The side that controls the narrative controls the verdict.

The phrase *One man's terrorist is another man's freedom fighter* is often dismissed as a moral dodge or a trite slogan. In truth, it captures something profound about the subjectivity of political violence. The same act, whether a bombing, a hijacking or a raid, can be framed as criminal, heroic, tragic or necessary.

History adds another layer. Those who were once branded as terrorists often become respected statesmen.

Michael Collins, once hunted by the British as a terrorist, is now celebrated as a founding father of Irish independence. Menachem Begin, once labelled a terrorist by the British for his role in the Irgun's campaign against British rule in Palestine, later became Prime Minister of Israel and a Nobel Peace Prize laureate. Martin McGuinness, once Chief of Staff of the IRA, became a statesman and peacemaker as Deputy First Minister of Northern Ireland. The label is not fixed. It is fluid. The tide that shifts it is political power.

**CONCLUSION: The Question That Guides This Book**

This book is about that tide. It explores how the term *terrorism* is used, abused, manipulated and deployed. It examines who gets to speak, who gets to label and who is silenced. It interrogates why some acts are immortalised in horror while others are quietly justified.

It is about narrative warfare, the fight not over what happened, but over what it is called. It is about law and propaganda, media and silence. It is about Wounded Knee, Gaza, Grozny, Baghdad and Belfast. It is about names etched on memorials and names erased from memory. It is about justice denied through vocabulary.

Because if violence is judged not by its nature but by its narrator, then what does the word *terrorist* truly mean, and who gets to decide?

# CHAPTER ONE:
# What's in a Name?

## Section 1: - How *terrorist* became the most powerful label in global politics

"Terrorist." Few words carry such immediate finality. It is a label that lands like a gavel strike, shutting down conversation, demanding condemnation and justifying retaliation. To be called a terrorist is to be cast outside the moral and legal order. The term confers a kind of pariah status from which there is no recovery and no appeal. But what does it mean, really, and who gets to decide?

The word itself is relatively modern in origin. It first gained prominence during the French Revolution, when the Jacobins proudly described themselves as *terrorists* while wielding state-sanctioned violence to root out enemies of the revolution. Far from being a term of scorn, it was initially worn as a badge of revolutionary virtue, a means to enforce moral and political purity through fear. Over time, however, the term shifted. It came to denote illegitimate violence, violence from below, violence by those not authorised by a state or crown. That evolution of meaning was no accident. It mirrored the growing consolidation of state power across the nineteenth and twentieth centuries.

By the time the twenty-first century arrived, "terrorism" had become the ultimate political slur. It was deployed not just against violent actors, but against movements, ideologies and sometimes even entire populations. The September 11 attacks in 2001 transformed the term from a niche descriptor into the linchpin of global security architecture. In the name of counterterrorism, governments passed sweeping laws, launched wars, detained people without trial and expanded surveillance to unprecedented levels. The word took on a magical quality. Simply labelling someone a terrorist was enough to strip them of rights, due process and even their humanity.

And yet, despite its extraordinary power, the word has no universally agreed definition. The United Nations has attempted for decades to codify a legal meaning, without success. States have their own lists, some contradictory. For instance, one country's *terrorist group* is another's strategic ally. The United States supported the Mujahideen in Afghanistan during the Cold War. Decades later, similar actors were deemed terrorists. Hamas, Hezbollah, the Kurdish PKK, the Tamil Tigers and even Nelson Mandela's ANC have, at various points, worn the terrorist label. Each has also been engaged with diplomatically by the very states that once vilified them.

This inconsistency is not a flaw in the system. It is the system. The power of the word *terrorist* lies precisely in its flexibility. It allows governments, militaries and media outlets to control the narrative. Two groups may use identical tactics, including bombings, kidnappings or guerrilla warfare, but only one will be called terrorists. The distinction is not in what they do, but in who they are and whether their cause aligns with or threatens established power.

Consider the coverage of Israeli and Palestinian violence. When an Israeli airstrike kills dozens of civilians in Gaza, it is framed as a defensive action or perhaps a regrettable error. When a Palestinian group fires a rocket, it is terrorism. The action, projecting lethal force towards civilians, is similar. But the framing differs widely. The state is presumed to have legitimacy, while the stateless, by default, do not. As a result, their actions are criminalised not just in deed, but in label.

The same double standard is evident in domestic politics. Black Lives Matter activists, climate protestors and even journalists have been smeared with the terrorist label. Meanwhile, white nationalist militias or right-wing extremists are often described in more sanitised terms: disturbed individuals, lone wolves or domestic extremists. The reluctance to apply the "T-word" to certain groups reveals its true purpose. It is not to describe behaviour, but to draw boundaries of moral legitimacy.

The consequences of this semantic sleight of hand are profound. Once a group or individual is branded a terrorist, normal rules no longer apply. Trials can be circumvented. Torture can be rationalised. Assassination becomes policy. In the aftermath of 9/11, the United States established a global network of black sites, detention centres and drone programmes, all justified under the rubric of counterterrorism. Guantánamo Bay remains a monument to what happens when language grants a licence to ignore law.

It is not just a matter of semantics. It is a matter of power. Language shapes perception, and perception shapes policy. As Orwell warned, political language is designed to make lies sound truthful and murder respectable. *Terrorist* is the most potent example of this tendency in the modern lexicon. It is a word that can end a life, a movement or a conversation.

And yet, we rarely stop to ask who defines it, who benefits from its use and what is lost when we allow such a powerful label to go unexamined.

In this chapter, and throughout this book, we will examine how the term has evolved, how it is used and abused, and how it functions not as a descriptor of violence but as a tool of power. For to understand what terrorism means in the twenty-first century, we must first understand who gets to use the word and why.

## Section 2: – The Most Powerful Word in Politics

"Terrorist." It is a word that ends conversations. It halts empathy, obliterates context, and closes off curiosity. In a single syllable, it renders motives irrelevant and debate redundant. Once uttered, it stamps the accused with a moral verdict so complete that no defence, no history, and no alternative lens can survive its shadow. This is the power of the label.

Across the globe, from Washington to Jerusalem, from Moscow to Beijing, this one word has shaped foreign policy, justified war, suspended civil liberties, and redefined friend and foe. And yet, for all its force, it is a word with no universal definition.

The United Nations, after decades of debate, still cannot agree on what exactly terrorism is. Legal scholars, intelligence agencies, human rights groups, and political leaders all offer definitions, but none are binding and many contradict one another. The Taliban were once terrorists, then negotiating partners, then de facto rulers. Nelson Mandela was branded a terrorist by the United States until 2008. Today, protesters in Western capitals and rebel fighters in occupied territories can be called terrorists or freedom fighters, depending entirely on who is holding the microphone.

This lack of consensus is not incidental. It is part of what makes the term so effective. Its ambiguity gives it elasticity. It can stretch to include almost any form of political violence, or exclude it if the politics suit. And that is the real story. The word *terrorist* is not about the act but about the actor. It is not descriptive. It is selective. It is not a neutral legal category; it is a weaponised designation deployed by the powerful.

## Section 3: – From the Gunpowder Plot to 9/11

Historically, the term *terrorism* has undergone multiple reincarnations. In the 18th century, during the French Revolution, *terror* was the name given to state violence. The Reign of Terror, led by Robespierre, used fear as a tool to control the masses. At the time, it was seen not as criminal but as necessary for revolutionary discipline.

By the 19th and early 20th centuries, anarchists and anti-colonial movements became the new face of terrorism in European discourse. The British labelled Irish republicans and Indian nationalists as terrorists, and the Russians did the same with dissidents and revolutionaries.

But it was the 11 September 2001 attacks that redefined the term for the 21st century. The image of two planes striking the Twin Towers became the definitive visual of *terror*. In its aftermath, terrorism became less about a tactic and more about a permanent threat, a worldview, an enemy without end.

In response, the United States declared a War on Terror, an abstract war against an undefined foe. It enabled indefinite detention, pre-emptive strikes, drone warfare, and domestic surveillance. It was the perfect war: borderless, timeless, and forever justified by fear. Other states followed suit. Russia framed Chechen separatists as terrorists, and China did the same with Uyghur Muslims. Israel applied the label to Palestinian resistance. The state narrative was set. *Terrorist* equals enemy of the state, and enemies of the state do not deserve rights.

## Section 4: – The Politics of Labelling

Who gets to decide what terrorism is? This is the foundational question. And the answer, almost always, is the state. States possess the power to legislate, define and enforce. They decide who is on the list and who is not. This list, while often cloaked in the language of law and security, is always political.

Take, for example, the case of Hamas. Recognised by some countries as a terrorist organisation, Hamas is simultaneously a political party, a social service provider and a de facto government in Gaza. Contrast this with the Israeli Defence Forces, whose military operations have killed thousands of civilians, including children, journalists and medics. One is terrorism. The other is defence. The distinction is not based on civilian deaths, but on who holds the narrative power.

When a state uses violence, it is often deemed legitimate. When non-state actors do the same, it is called terrorism. This is not a comment on morality, but on framing. The act may be identical, a bombing, a targeted killing or a blockade, but the label changes the meaning. And once the label is applied, the conversation changes.

## Section 5: – Media, Myth, and Manufactured Consent

Media plays a central role in this ecosystem of labelling. It amplifies state narratives, often without scrutiny. Headlines scream *terrorist attack* before any investigation is complete. News anchors repeat government talking points. Editors shape public sentiment by choosing which deaths to mourn and which to ignore.

The result is a form of manufactured consent. The public is conditioned to accept state violence as necessary and to view non-state violence as an existential threat. This binary simplifies complex political struggles into good versus evil, hero versus villain, democracy versus terror.

But the reality is rarely that clear. Often, those labelled as terrorists are fighting against occupation, dictatorship or systemic injustice. Their violence may be reprehensible, but so too may be the conditions that gave rise to it. The media, however, seldom tells that part of the story. Nuance does not sell.

## Section 6: - Power Decides, Language Obscures

In the end, the label *terrorist* is not about clarity, but about control. It is about who gets to speak and who must be silenced. It is about which lives are grievable and which are disposable. It is about the right to resist and the right to repress.

Terrorism is real. It has taken countless lives and caused immeasurable suffering. But so too has state violence cloaked in the language of law and order. To challenge the label is not to excuse the violence, it is to interrogate the narrative.

As we proceed through this book, one question will keep reappearing. If violence is judged not by its nature but by its narrator, then what does the word *terrorist* truly mean, and who gets to decide?

# CHAPTER TWO

## Section 1: - The Myth of a Single Definition

Ask ten people what terrorism means and you will likely get ten different answers. Some might point to 9/11. Others to a suicide bombing in a crowded market. A few might name groups such as Hamas, ISIS, the IRA or al-Qaeda. Others still might talk about lone wolves with guns or trucks or manifestos. The word conjures immediate imagery and emotion, but ask for a definition and suddenly the conversation stalls. What exactly is terrorism? Is it defined by the act, the motive, the target or the perpetrator?

For all its ubiquity in headlines, speeches and political debate, terrorism remains one of the most poorly defined terms in modern discourse. There is no universally accepted legal definition, not in international law, not at the United Nations, not even within some countries themselves. The UN has been trying, and failing, for decades to reach a consensus. Every draft falters on the same point: disagreement over whether violent resistance by occupied or stateless peoples, especially in struggles of national liberation, should be included or exempt.

The United States and its allies, for instance, have long resisted any definition that might limit their military operations abroad. At the same time, many developing nations argue that national liberation movements, such as the ANC during apartheid South Africa or the PLO in the 1980s, should never be placed alongside groups like al-Qaeda. For decades, this stalemate has persisted. The result is chaos. One man's terrorist is another man's freedom fighter.

This ambiguity is not just academic. It bleeds into the real world, into how laws are written, how wars are justified and how people are prosecuted or protected. Governments decide who is labelled a terrorist and who is not. That power to define is also a power to control. Label a group as terrorists and you shut down conversation, eliminate nuance and justify violence. Label the same group as freedom fighters and suddenly their actions, however bloody, are cast in a very different light.

Consider the Afghan Mujahideen in the 1980s. When they were fighting the Soviets, the West armed and praised them. When some of those same fighters became part of the Taliban, the label changed overnight, from brave warriors to terrorists. The actions did not always change, but the narrative did.

Or take Nelson Mandela. Once considered a terrorist by both the UK and US, his African National Congress was subjected to surveillance and travel bans. Even as late as 2008, Mandela was still on a US terrorist watch list. Today he is an icon of peace. What changed was not the man, but the context, the politics and the power to tell the story.

This slipperiness gives the term a unique kind of utility. Politicians can wield it like a club to crush opponents, silence dissent or justify war. Because there is no universal standard, they are rarely challenged. The word terrorism carries a moral clarity that other legal terms do not. It evokes fear, horror and condemnation. Yet its meaning is shaped far more by who says it than by what actually happened.

So why is there no agreed definition? Partly it is because of the word's inherent political volatility. Any attempt to define terrorism immediately raises uncomfortable questions about state violence, military intervention and historic wrongs. If you include the killing of civilians for political ends, then do drone strikes that kill children qualify? What about economic sanctions that cause famine and death? What about the bombings of Hiroshima and Nagasaki?

Most nations would prefer not to have that conversation. They want a definition that includes their enemies but not themselves.

Even academics have struggled. In 1988, political scientist Alex P. Schmid surveyed more than 100 definitions and identified 22 different elements common among them, but no single, agreed combination. In fact, the only element they all shared was violence or the threat of violence. Beyond that, everything else, from motive to target to legitimacy, was open to debate.

That ambiguity has only widened over time, as terrorism has shifted from coordinated insurgencies to lone actors, from religious zealots to political extremists, from bombings to cyberattacks. In today's world, terrorism is as much about perception and media framing as it is about death tolls or tactics. A mass shooting by a white nationalist might be called a hate crime. A similar attack by a Muslim might be called terrorism. The facts could be identical, yet the narrative is not.

This leads to a deeply uncomfortable question. If we cannot define terrorism consistently, how can we fight it justly?

## Section 2: - A Term Without Borders

If terrorism resists definition, it also resists containment. It crosses borders not only physically but conceptually. Over time, the term has metastasised and has been applied not only to groups with bombs and guns but to protest movements, ideological enemies and even dissident individuals. In the absence of a universal legal framework, the label can be, and often is, weaponised by states and regimes across the globe.

Russia has branded Alexei Navalny's anti-corruption network as extremist, a close cousin to terrorism under Russian law, effectively outlawing dissent. China uses counter-terror rhetoric to justify its mass internment of Uyghurs in Xinjiang, painting religious expression and cultural identity as threats to state security. In Israel, Palestinian resistance is frequently labelled terrorism, even when it involves stone-throwing teenagers or journalists. In the United States, peaceful protests have been treated with the full weight of anti-terror law depending on who is protesting and what they are protesting for.

This is no accident. It is the result of a term that lacks a centre. Without a shared definition, terrorism becomes whatever those in power say it is. It has no inherent meaning, only applied meaning. That is profoundly dangerous.

Think about the word in another context. Imagine if murder had no universal definition. Imagine if it meant different things in every country. Imagine if some states defined it as premeditated killing while others defined it as political dissent. Imagine if courts were allowed to convict people of murder without needing to prove that death had occurred. That is the legal chaos we face with terrorism.

Even where definitions exist, they are often broad to the point of absurdity. In Egypt, individuals have been convicted of terrorism for spreading false news. In the UK, counter-terrorism powers have been used to detain climate activists and journalists. In the United States, the FBI has controversially surveilled Black Lives Matter organisers under domestic terrorism guidelines, despite no evidence of organised violence.

Then there are the laws that exist only in name, with no due process at all. Guantanamo Bay stands as the ultimate symbol of legal black holes, where individuals labelled terrorists by the US government have been held for decades without trial. Some were swept up by bounty hunters, handed over without evidence and tortured based on suspicion. The term terrorist was enough to erase rights, silence international outcry and indefinitely delay justice.

The inconsistency is not limited to the law. It also infects international diplomacy. Nations who bomb civilians are condemned unless they are allies. Groups that resist occupation are called terrorists unless they serve the interests of powerful states. One man's proxy is another man's insurgent. One country's peacekeeping mission is another's occupation.

Terrorism, in short, has become a floating signifier, a word that attaches itself to enemies but never to allies, to out-groups but never to the in-group, to the powerless but rarely to the powerful.

This is how the word has been used to crush liberation movements and sanctify military empires. This is how a state can launch a missile that kills a family and call it a surgical strike, while a homemade explosive that injures a soldier is labelled terrorism. It is not the act. It is the actor.

It is why Benjamin Netanyahu can publicly insist that Palestinians do not have the right to self-defence. That statement, made without irony, is rooted in the asymmetric logic of the terrorism label. Israel defends itself. Palestinians terrorise. Full stop. Even when bombs fall on hospitals or refugee camps, the justification, self-defence, is accepted almost uncritically by Western powers.

It is also why, when Netanyahu accused UNRWA, the United Nations Relief and Works Agency for Palestinian refugees, of aiding terrorism because some of its staff allegedly had links to Hamas, entire Western governments defunded the agency without trial, review or evidence. This is the power of guilt by association, a recurring theme throughout this book.

If terrorism were a crime based purely on actions, we might come closer to justice. But it is not. It is a narrative tool. It allows states to claim the moral high ground, to justify violence, to excuse civilian deaths and to label their enemies as monsters. It has become a currency, traded for legitimacy, sympathy and power.

Perhaps most dangerously, it enables impunity. Once a state claims it is fighting terrorism, it can suspend normal rules. Habeas corpus can vanish. Torture can be justified. Airstrikes can be declared necessary. Civilian casualties become a sad inevitability. All of this is cloaked in the language of righteousness.

In this context, terrorism is no longer about what is done. It is about who is doing it and to whom. In that framing, the law becomes not a tool of justice but a reflection of power.

## Section 3: - The Politics of Exemption

There are two sets of rules in the global conversation about violence. One applies to states and the other to everyone else.

When a state launches a missile that levels a block of flats, we are told it is an unfortunate tragedy, an accident, a defensive necessity or a mistake in targeting. When a stateless actor plants a crude explosive under a military convoy, it is condemned, almost universally, as an act of terrorism. Yet the impact on human life is often the same. The distinction lies not in the action but in the actor. From that single difference flows an entire doctrine of moral exemption.

Take, for instance, Israel's treatment of Palestinians, a case that lays bare the full hypocrisy of the system. In October 2023, the world watched as Gaza was bombed relentlessly following the 7 October Hamas attacks. Civilian homes, hospitals and schools were hit with precision and repetition. Water and electricity were cut. Medical supplies were blocked. Whole neighbourhoods were reduced to rubble. Thousands were killed, many of them children. Independent human rights bodies have since called it a war crime. Some have even used the word genocide.

But not terrorism.

Why not? If the same acts were carried out by an armed militia, bombing schools, cutting off water and killing civilians, there would be no hesitation. The word terrorism would be used by every major government and media outlet in the West. But because these acts were committed by a state, one closely aligned with Western interests, a different language is applied: military response, targeted operations, legitimate self-defence.

This is the politics of exemption in action.

And it is not just about Israel. The United States, for example, has conducted thousands of drone strikes across sovereign borders in countries with which it is not at war, including Pakistan, Somalia and Yemen. In 2015, a US drone strike in Yemen killed thirteen civilians in a wedding convoy. In 2020, another drone strike killed an Afghan aid worker and seven children. The Pentagon later admitted it got it wrong, yet there were no sanctions, no charges and no accusations of terrorism. Only silence.

When the state kills, it is presumed to be for good reason. When others kill, it is presumed to be evil. This is the unspoken rule that governs the global discourse on terrorism. It is rooted not in law or morality, but in power.

Benjamin Netanyahu, when asked by a journalist whether Palestinians had the right to defend themselves, famously replied, 'No.' That blunt answer exposed a core principle of this doctrine. Some people and some nations are allowed to defend themselves. Others are not. Some are allowed to retaliate. Others are expected to suffer quietly. If they resist, they are branded as extremists, militants, radicals or terrorists.

Gideon Levy, the Israeli journalist long critical of his government, has pointed out that part of the problem lies in the belief that Israelis are God's Chosen People, a belief that, in practice, has created a mindset of legal and moral exemption. If one truly believes their people are uniquely ordained, then the rules that apply to others become optional. International law, human rights conventions and even the Geneva Conventions become rules for other people, not for the exceptional.

That belief has real-world consequences. It means Israel can blockade Gaza for more than a decade, restrict medical supplies, deny exit permits to cancer patients and bomb schools and refugee camps, all while insisting it is acting in accordance with international law. And the world, largely, allows it to happen.

But let us be honest. Israel is not alone in claiming exceptionalism. The United States has long seen itself as the moral authority in global affairs, even as it engages in activities that, by any neutral standard, would qualify as terrorism. Torture, targeted killings, secret prisons, regime change and civilian casualties dismissed as collateral damage are all examples.

If any other nation carried out these acts, it would face condemnation, sanctions and possibly war crimes trials. But when the United States does it, it is policy. It is strategy. It is part of the War on Terror.

The irony, of course, is that the War on Terror has itself produced a staggering amount of what many would reasonably call terror. Bombings, displacements, mass detentions and indefinite imprisonment have all been carried out in the name of fighting terrorism. The label has become so elastic, and so dependent on who is doing the speaking, that it no longer describes an act. It describes an identity. You are a terrorist not because of what you do, but because of who you are in the eyes of those with power.

And who is not labelled a terrorist? That is often more revealing.

In the early days of the conflict in Ukraine, Western media was filled with stories of bravery, resistance and national pride. Molotov cocktails were made in schools and passed around by grandmothers. Civilians armed themselves and set up ambushes. They were praised, respected and celebrated. That was not terrorism, we were told. It was freedom fighting.

And it was. But imagine if the same headlines had come out of Baghdad in 2004, or Gaza in 2023, or Kabul in 2021. Imagine civilians taking up arms against occupying forces, sabotaging tanks and launching improvised weapons. Would they be heroes? Or would they be insurgents, militants or extremists?

Language does the work of propaganda. It creates heroes or villains. The choice often has nothing to do with the violence committed, but with the politics of who is allowed to resist and who is not. The politics of exemption is not accidental. It is the foundation of the global security architecture. It protects powerful nations from the legal consequences of their violence while simultaneously granting them the authority to define the violence of others.

This asymmetry is deeply corrosive. It tells the world that international law is not universal but selective. That human rights depend not on principle but on alliance. That some lives are mourned while others are measured.

If we are to reclaim the word terrorism as something meaningful, we must dismantle the politics of exemption. We must ask not who committed the violence, but what the violence was. We must hold all actors to the same standards or none at all. Because as long as the powerful remain exempt, the powerless will always be criminalised and justice will remain out of reach.

## Section 4: - The Slippery Slope of Self-Defence

The most universally accepted justification for violence is self-defence. It is written into international law, enshrined in national constitutions, and woven into the moral fabric of human instinct. If someone comes to harm you or your family, you have a right to protect yourself. Nations claim the same right.

But what happens when that right becomes a shield for unchecked power, or worse, a sword for pre-emptive violence?

In theory, self-defence is reactive: a proportional response to an imminent threat. In practice, the term has been stretched, twisted and distorted beyond recognition. It has become a default justification for almost any act of state violence, no matter how aggressive, disproportionate or far removed from the original threat. The slope is slippery, and most of the world is already quite a way down that slide.

Let us recall the 2003 invasion of Iraq. The US and UK governments framed it not as an act of aggression, but as necessary self-defence against weapons of mass destruction, a claim that turned out to be completely false. No WMDs were found. No active threat existed. Yet hundreds of thousands of Iraqi civilians died, a nation was destabilised, and the groundwork was laid for the rise of ISIS. Was that self-defence, or was it conquest under a semi-legal veil?

The government of Israel has long relied on the doctrine of self-defence to justify its military actions, even those that appear offensive in nature. Following the cross-border assault by Hamas on 7 October 2023, an attack in which around 1,200 Israelis were killed, a defensive operation was declared. Over 65,000 Palestinians have since lost their lives, many of them civilians. Entire neighbourhoods have been levelled. Hospitals, schools and refugee camps have been bombed. Yet the refrain from Western leaders remains unflinching: "Israel has the right to defend itself."

What is far less widely acknowledged is how Israel's own military doctrine may have contributed to the scale of death, even among its own citizens. A July 2024 investigation by *Haaretz* found that the Israeli Defence Forces invoked the Hannibal Directive, a controversial and previously retired order that authorised troops to use any means necessary to prevent the capture of soldiers, including heavy fire even at the risk of friendly fire or civilian casualties, during the chaos of 7 October. One message retrieved by *Haaretz* from early that morning simply states, "Hannibal at Erez" followed by "dispatch a Zik [attack drone]."

The directive, originally revoked in 2016, reappeared in the operational orders of the Gaza Division in the early hours of the attack. The order "Not a single vehicle can return to Gaza" was transmitted minutes later, even though many of the vehicles were believed to be carrying both hostages and civilians.

If the doctrine of self-defence underpins Israel's moral and legal posture, the invocation of the Hannibal Directive clouds that narrative. When a military claims to act defensively yet simultaneously issues orders that may endanger its own people and largely civilian populations, the boundaries between offence and protection blur. The violence that follows, whether from the enemy or from the state itself, becomes diplomatically legitimised, even when it contradicts the very notion of self-defence.

In this case, the label of terror and the rhetoric of defence serve as shields, not only for state action but for the erasure of responsibility. The question then is not simply who attacked, but who defined defence, and how many lives were sacrificed in its name.

And defend from what: civilians? Children? Cancer patients in besieged hospitals?

The concept of self-defence has lost its shape. It is no longer a narrowly defined, proportional act. It has become an open-ended mandate, a blank cheque. The state need only assert it and suddenly all moral scrutiny is suspended.

Even pre-emptive violence now wears the cloak of self-defence. The so-called Bush Doctrine made this explicit: strike first, justify later. If there is a perceived threat, even one in the future, the state reserves the right to kill. The logic is terrifyingly circular. If an enemy might attack one day, then attacking them first becomes an act of defence. The burden of proof evaporates. Suspicion, even rumour, becomes sufficient.

Under this logic, nearly any act of violence can be justified. Assassinations. Drone strikes. Economic sanctions that kill civilians through starvation or medical shortages. All wrapped in the language of defence. But is starving a population self-defence or state terrorism? Is bombing an apartment block self-defence or state terrorism? At what point does it become what it really is ... terrorism?

The problem is not merely linguistic; it is political. Once an act is classified as self-defence, it becomes immune to critique. It is no longer violence, it is necessity. No longer a choice, it is a right. That reclassification has consequences. It shuts down investigation, criminal accountability and media scrutiny. It allows states to act with impunity while claiming victimhood.

This logic infects media narratives, too. When a state with geopolitical clout bombs a village, the headlines read, "Airstrike Targets Militants." When the victims turn out to be children, the terminology shifts to "collateral damage." When the attacker is non-state, the language hardens: "Terrorists kill civilians in deadly blast." One is an accident; the other is evil. But is a dead child any less dead because a uniformed air force dropped the bomb?

The United Nations Charter recognises the right to self-defence in Article 51, but with strict conditions: it must be in response to an armed attack and reported to the Security Council. Yet few states follow this protocol. Instead, they act unilaterally, offer vague justifications and let the media and allies do the rest.

So, is this self-defence or, more accurately, narrative warfare?

It is not only major powers. Smaller states have adopted the same rhetorical playbook. Saudi Arabia justifies its brutal war in Yemen as self-defence against Houthi rebels. Russia claimed its invasion of Ukraine was necessary to defend ethnic Russians in the Donbas. Turkey labels Kurdish groups as existential threats to justify cross-border strikes into Syria. India frames its crackdowns in Kashmir as counterterrorism. In each case, violence is painted as virtue.

But self-defence without accountability is indistinguishable from aggression.

A more disturbing development is the shift towards collective punishment in the name of self-defence. The logic here is simple: if a terrorist group operates within a population, then the population itself is complicit. This rationale was used in the bombings of Fallujah, the sieges of Gaza and the destruction of entire districts in Aleppo. The innocent are reclassified as human shields or sympathisers. Once that mental switch is flipped, almost anything becomes permissible.

This is not to say self-defence is invalid. Nations do face threats. Civilians are killed by terrorist groups. Governments must respond. But the response must be judged not by who delivers it, but by what is done. In too many cases, the actions taken in defence far exceed any moral or legal justification.

It is not self-defence to kill indiscriminately. It is not self-defence to target civilian infrastructure. It is not self-defence to occupy, to starve or to bomb without regard for human life. These are acts of terror and violence, and no slogan, no matter how familiar, can absolve them.

As long as self-defence is allowed to mean whatever a state wants it to mean, the international order remains broken. And the word *terrorism* will continue to be selectively applied, and never to those with the power to define the terms.

## Section 5: - Drone Warfare – Death Without a Face

There is something eerily antiseptic about modern warfare. Gone are the muddy trenches, the bayonets, the battlefield cries. Today, war is often waged from air-conditioned bunkers thousands of miles away. A joystick is pushed, a target is marked, and a missile is dispatched from a drone hovering silently above. The result is death delivered by algorithm. Precision killing, they call it. Targeted assassination. No boots on the ground, no flag-draped coffins, just an explosion in a village far away, followed by a statement: "A suspected militant has been neutralised."

But who decides who that "militant" is? Who confirms the intelligence? Who counts the bodies afterwards? And perhaps most importantly, what happens when we no longer see the people we kill?

Drone warfare is the clearest example of how the modern state has sanitised violence. It removes the human cost not from the victims, but from the perpetrators. The drone operator does not hear the screams or see the limbs scattered. They see a screen. A pixel cluster. A heat signature. And when the strike is done, they go home to dinner. The dissonance is built into the system. It is not war, it is software.

Since the early 2000s, the United States has become the world's foremost proponent of drone warfare. Under Presidents Bush, Obama, Trump and Biden, the drone programme expanded from isolated strikes to a routine method of targeted killing. Pakistan, Yemen, Somalia, Afghanistan and Libya, the list of countries where drones have killed without formal war declarations grows by the year. And in nearly every case, the strikes are justified under the banner of counter-terrorism.

The irony, of course, is that the act itself, extrajudicial killing without trial, often in sovereign nations, resulting in civilian casualties, fits many if not most of the definitions of terrorism. It is politically motivated violence. It creates fear. It is targeted. It is lethal. But because it is done by a state, with formalised protocols and a clean kill report, it is accepted. Even praised. Yet if a non-state actor blew up a wedding, a hospital or a home from the sky, it would be called exactly what it is: terrorism.

Take the infamous case of the 2010 drone strike in Yemen that killed Anwar al-Awlaki, an American citizen accused of encouraging jihadist attacks. He was never formally charged or tried. Two weeks later, his sixteen-year-old son, also a U.S. citizen, was killed in a separate strike while eating dinner with his cousins. No evidence linked the teenager to any crime. When pressed, a White House official said coldly, "He should have had a more responsible father."

And there you have it. That was the logic. Guilt by relation. Death without trial. Yet not terrorism, apparently.

According to the independent watchdog group Airwars, thousands of civilians have died in drone strikes over the past two decades. Children. Women. First responders who rushed to the scene of an initial blast only to be killed by a second, what the military calls a "double tap". How clinical. This tactic, common in drone operations, would be classed as a war crime if done by any other actor. When Hamas does it, it is evil. When the CIA does it, it is classified.

The opacity of drone warfare is part of its appeal to states. There is no footage, no embedded journalists, no public funerals. Bodies are reduced to metadata. Mistakes are described as "regrettable". And when those mistakes are challenged, for example in the August 2021 drone strike in Kabul that killed ten innocent civilians, including seven children, the Pentagon issues a brief report and moves on. No charges. No accountability. No justice.

Yet the consequences ripple far beyond the immediate blast zone. Drone warfare fuels anti-Western resentment, radicalises survivors, and erodes the moral high ground that democracies claim to hold. It is the perfect example of violence without proximity, killing stripped of consequence.

Even the soldiers operating these drones suffer. PTSD among drone pilots is well documented. The human brain cannot compartmentalise death quite so easily. Watching someone for days, learning their routines, then pressing a button and watching their life end leaves a mark. And when that person turns out to be innocent, that mark becomes a scar.

Yet despite all this, drone use continues to grow. Other nations have followed America's lead. Israel has used drones extensively in Gaza. Turkey deploys them in Syria and against Kurdish fighters. Iran develops its own variants. Russia has used them in Ukraine. China sells them on the open market. We are entering a new age of remote warfare, one where any nation can become a silent assassin in the sky.

With the rise of autonomous drones, AI-powered weapons that can identify and strike targets without human intervention, the dangers multiply. Who programs the algorithm? Who defines "hostile"? What safeguards exist when the line between enemy combatant and civilian is already so blurred?

This is the future of warfare: no warning, no trial, no accountability.

And yet, the terrorism label is never applied. Why? Because terrorism, we are told, is something done by others. By them. Never by us.

The unsettling reality is that the most advanced forms of violence in the world today, precise, unaccountable, state sanctioned, are exempt from scrutiny because they wear the cloak of legitimacy. A cloak made not of morality, but of narrative. We are defending ourselves, the states say. We are neutralising threats. We are keeping the world safe.

But to the people on the ground, to the families turned to ash and the children buried in rubble, does it matter whether the missile was fired by a rebel or by a military operating under a flag?

Death is death.

And when it comes without warning, without evidence, without trial and without remorse, it is not defence. It is not justice. And if we called it by its real name, perhaps the world would see it for what it is. Terrorism.

## Section 6: - Starvation, Siege, and Sanctions – Violence by Deprivation

In the modern age, violence, or indeed terrorism, no longer needs bullets or bombs. It can come in the form of hunger. It can arrive quietly, wrapped in bureaucracy, dressed as policy, and it can wear the badge of international diplomacy or domestic necessity. But its effects are unmistakable: malnourished children, crumbling hospitals, economic collapse and desperation. And yet, when states use starvation as a weapon, or impose sieges that deny people the essentials of life, the word terrorism rarely enters the conversation.

Why? Because this is not seen as violence. It is seen as strategy.

Sanctions. Blockades. Import restrictions. Freezing of assets. The cutting off of electricity, water, fuel or food. These are tools used by governments, not against soldiers on a battlefield, but against populations. Civilian populations. Entire cities. Even entire countries.

And yet the moral outrage that follows a suicide bombing or hostage taking is seldom echoed when thousands die slowly from engineered famine or medical deprivation.

Gaza illustrates this perfectly, a stretch of land so tightly controlled that UN officials have referred to it as an "open-air prison". For more than a decade, Israel's blockade has choked access to food, medicine, construction materials, fuel and even water. Fishing zones have been restricted. Electricity is often limited to just a few hours per day. In 2012, a leaked Israeli policy document revealed a calculation of the minimum number of calories Gazans would need to avoid malnutrition, a literal measurement of how tightly the population could be squeezed without technically triggering famine.

In any other context, this would be called what it is: collective punishment. A siege. A slow and deliberate act of deprivation targeting civilians for the political aims of the powerful. A war crime.

When Hamas fires rockets, it is labelled terrorism, immediately and unequivocally. But when an entire population is denied cancer treatments because chemotherapy drugs are deemed a "dual use" threat, the moral framework collapses. The suffering becomes abstract. The victims become statistics.

And this double standard is not confined to the Middle East.

In Yemen, the Saudi-led blockade, supported by U.S. logistics and weaponry, has helped create one of the worst humanitarian crises in the world. Hospitals without fuel. Markets without food. More than 150,000 people have died in the conflict, including tens of thousands of children from starvation. But because it is done through official channels, backed by UN resolutions and military alliances, the terrorism label is never invoked. It is a war, they say. A legitimate one. Yet are the people any less terrorised?

And yet if a non-state actor were to cut off food to an entire city, block medical supplies, and prevent the sick from leaving for treatment, it would be front page news. There would be condemnations. Demands for justice. Perhaps even drone strikes in retaliation.

But when it is a state, it becomes geopolitics. Policy. National interest.

Sanctions, too, have become a favoured weapon of economic war. They are touted as humane alternatives to military intervention. But are they?

Look at Iraq in the 1990s. The sanctions imposed after the Gulf War decimated the country's infrastructure. Hospitals could not get equipment. Water treatment facilities broke down. By the end of the decade, UNICEF estimated that more than 500,000 Iraqi children had died as a result. Five hundred thousand children. When the then U.S. Secretary of State Madeleine Albright was asked in 1996 whether the price was worth it, she replied, infamously, "We think the price is worth it." And again, there you have it. But who is the "we"? Certainly not those innocents who suffered the terrorism of the policy.

Imagine a non-state group making such a claim. Imagine the outcry.

Sanctions on Iran, Venezuela, Syria and North Korea have similarly affected ordinary citizens far more than the elites they were meant to pressure. Food prices rise. Medicine becomes scarce. Infant mortality increases. Chronic illness goes untreated. Desperation breeds unrest. Yet this is seen as leverage, not cruelty.

And the most grotesque irony is that these acts are often done in the name of human rights.

We are starving you to help you. We are blocking your hospitals to liberate you. We are isolating your economy to protect the world.

In many ways, siege and starvation tactics are more insidious than overt violence. They leave no dramatic headlines. They do not involve suicide bombers or televised explosions. Yet they achieve the same ends: death, fear, submission, terror. And because the harm is slow, statistical and bureaucratic, the perpetrators escape moral scrutiny.

No terrorist group has ever killed as many people through deprivation as state imposed sieges or sanctions. Yet one is universally condemned; the other is debated at G7 meetings and wrapped in press releases. The politics of language shields the state. A starving child in Gaza or Yemen dies not at the hands of a bomb, but at the hands of paperwork. Of border closures. Of asset freezes. Of legalese.

But does the method matter to the dead?

When states weaponise scarcity, when they deliberately induce suffering not to defeat armies but to break the spirit of a people, it is not strategy. It is terror by another name. And if we are to be honest, we must admit that the victims are the same. Only the uniforms change.

## Section 7: - The Gaza Paradox – When Genocide Isn't Terrorism

Gaza is the paradox that breaks the frame.

Here is a place where entire apartment blocks are flattened in seconds, where hospitals are reduced to rubble, where journalists, medics, aid workers and children die beneath drone-fired missiles, and yet, somehow, it is not labelled terrorism. Not even when it fits every common-sense description of the word.

In Gaza, we see civilians killed en masse. We see fear weaponised. We see a people terrorised. And yet the violence remains quarantined under another name: defence, war, collateral damage. Anything but terrorism.

Why?

Because the actor is a state. And, more importantly, it is a Western ally.

The scale of destruction in Gaza since 2007 defies belief. During the 2014 conflict alone, more than 2,000 Palestinians were killed, more than 500 of them children. In the 2021 bombardment, entire families were wiped out in a single airstrike. In 2023, a strike on the Jabalia refugee camp levelled residential blocks, killing dozens. And in 2025, the world watched again as Israeli warplanes pounded Gaza in retaliation for Hamas attacks, this time with even less restraint, fewer humanitarian pauses and a declared intent to eliminate the threat permanently.

That phrase, eliminate the threat, echoes in every justification for state violence. But in Gaza, it translates to the mass killing of civilians under the guise of precision warfare.

Israel, of course, insists it targets only militants, that Hamas embeds itself within civilian populations, that every school, hospital or mosque struck was being used by terrorists. But if the claim is always that terrorists are hiding behind civilians, then every civilian death becomes the terrorists' fault. Every corpse becomes a necessary cost. Every child becomes a human shield. It is a framing so powerful it absolves the state of any accountability.

And yet the numbers tell a different story.

Thousands of civilians. Hundreds of children. Vital infrastructure destroyed. Power plants bombed. UN facilities struck. Humanitarian convoys hit. And in 2024, for the first time, leading human rights bodies, including the UN, began to use a different word for what was happening: genocide.

Genocide, the deliberate destruction of a people. The erasure of their homes, their dignity, their very survival.

And still… not terrorism.

In some conflicts, the veil of strategic ambiguity or security necessity is used to obscure true intent. But in the case of Israel's assault on Gaza, even that veil has at times been stripped away. The language of terror has not only been used against Palestinians, it has been owned, endorsed and escalated by senior Israeli officials.

On 8 July 2025, Israeli Minister of National Security Itamar Ben Gvir declared: "They should be crushed to pieces, starved to death and not resuscitated with humanitarian aid that gives them oxygen." Finance Minister Bezalel Smotrich, doubling down, stated unequivocally: "We will never allow a single grain of wheat to enter the Gaza Strip," later suggesting it might be "justified to let 2 million Palestinians die of hunger." Meanwhile, Heritage Minister Amichai Ben Eliyahu dismissed even death as insufficient, stating that "the army must find ways more painful than death for the civilians in Gaza. Killing them is not enough."

These are not isolated provocations. They are declarations of intent, issued from the highest levels of government, articulating a strategy that not only permits but encourages mass civilian suffering. When such rhetoric is given political legitimacy, it is no longer simply war. It is a campaign of terror by design.

This is the paradox. When a state inflicts terror on a people, the world reaches for softer terms. It invokes law. It seeks balance. It examines context. The state is given space to explain itself, to reframe, to soften the edges. Meanwhile, when Hamas fires rockets, or a Palestinian stabs a settler, the word terrorist is applied instantly, with moral clarity and no further inquiry.

Benjamin Netanyahu was once asked directly if Palestinians had a right to defend themselves. His answer was a cold, unequivocal no. Not just Hamas. Not militants. All Palestinians. The implication was clear: only Israel may strike. Only Israel may claim victimhood. Any resistance, no matter how symbolic or desperate, is terror.

And in this framing, everything becomes permissible, and we are witnessing the outworking of that.

Gaza's children grow up surrounded by drones. Its parents bury their families beneath rubble. Medical teams operate without anaesthetic. And still, the world debates whether it is proportional, whether it is justified, whether Israel has the right to defend itself. But no one asks if Gaza has the right to survive, much less defend themselves.

When the International Criminal Court began investigating war crimes in the Palestinian territories, Israeli officials responded with outrage. How dare they? Israel, they insisted, was being singled out, targeted unfairly. But this, too, reveals the paradox. When your acts are defined not by what you do, but by who you are, any scrutiny becomes persecution.

UNRWA, the primary humanitarian agency serving Palestinians, was defunded in 2024 after Israel accused several staff members of ties to Hamas. No evidence was presented publicly. No trial occurred. But the association alone, the suspicion, was enough to cut off food, medicine and shelter to more than a million people. Guilt by association is powerful. It punishes entire populations. And when applied from a position of power, it never triggers the label of terrorism.

Now consider this. If a stateless group used siege, starvation, airstrikes and targeted assassinations to control a population, would they be called anything but terrorists?

Would we accept explanations of defence?

Would we praise their restraint?

Would we fund them?

Or would we, rightly, recoil?

The Gaza Paradox reveals the fundamental flaw in our global understanding of terrorism. It is not defined by suffering. It is not defined by violence. It is defined by power, who holds it and who narrates the story.

As Israeli journalist Gideon Levy once asked: Are we a people for whom no law applies? His question was not rhetorical. It was a challenge to the double standards that shield the powerful from accountability.

When the state becomes the perpetrator, the rules are suspended. The moral compass spins. And genocide is not called terrorism, not because it is not, but because it is inconvenient to say so.

This is the Gaza Paradox. A place where terror rains from the sky but never receives the name it deserves. A place where words are more tightly policed than bombs, where one side's humanity is always questioned and the other's never.

And if we cannot name terror when it comes from the powerful, what is the point of naming it at all?

## Section 8: - Historical Amnesia – From Wounded Knee to My Lai

*History will remember what the powerful allow it to.*

When violence is state sanctioned, it is rarely remembered as terrorism. More often, it is repackaged as patriotism, reframed as security or simply forgotten altogether. This selective memory, what we might call historical amnesia, is not accidental. It is how the myth of legitimacy is maintained. It is how states protect themselves from the same moral scrutiny they so freely impose on others.

Take the Wounded Knee Massacre of 1890. Hundreds of Lakota Sioux were slaughtered by the US 7th Cavalry, many of them unarmed women and children. The dead were frozen in the snow for days. Their only crime was participating in a spiritual movement that white authorities feared. And yet the soldiers who carried out the massacre were not condemned. They were decorated. Twenty Medals of Honour were issued, the highest award for military valour in the United States.

In 2025, when asked whether those medals should finally be rescinded, US Secretary of Defence Pete Hegseth replied firmly: "No." He argued that they were awarded within the standards of the time. He dismissed criticism as a revisionist attack on American history. A review panel backed him.

So the slaughter remains honourable. A war crime becomes an act of national service. And those who committed it become heroes.

But what if the same act had been carried out by an Indigenous resistance group?

Would it still be celebrated?

Would their names appear on monuments or watch lists?

Would they be draped in medals, or hanged as terrorists?

This is the grotesque duality of how we remember violence. When the state commits it, it becomes part of heritage. When the oppressed commit it, it becomes a threat to civilisation.

The My Lai Massacre in Vietnam offers another chilling example. In 1968, US troops gunned down more than 500 unarmed villagers, mostly women, children and the elderly. The attack was systematic: people herded into ditches and executed, villages torched and bodies mutilated. The brutality was undeniable, even American soldiers were horrified.

And yet only one man, Lieutenant William Calley, was convicted. He served a mere three years under house arrest. President Nixon later commuted his sentence. There were no broader prosecutions, no branding of terrorism, no apology from the state.

Contrast this with the treatment of Vietnamese resistance fighters, labelled Viet Cong terrorists regardless of whether they attacked soldiers or infrastructure. The term did not depend on tactics, it depended on allegiance. One side committed atrocities but was granted legal cover. The other fought occupation and was condemned as barbaric.

In Northern Ireland, too, the past is a battleground of memory. The Special Powers Act, introduced in 1922, gave the British state sweeping authority to detain without trial, ban publications and outlaw organisations. It created a two tier justice system. Irish nationalists, many protesting against discrimination and inequality, were criminalised and labelled as threats. Meanwhile, state sanctioned violence, including the actions of undercover operatives and paramilitary collusion, was rarely scrutinised.

The legacy continues. To this day, the British government resists investigations into its actions during the Troubles while prosecuting former IRA members. Memory, it seems, is selective and weaponised.

Israel again offers a contemporary parallel. In 1948, more than 700,000 Palestinians were expelled or fled from their homes in what they call the Nakba, the catastrophe. Villages were razed. Families never returned. Armed Jewish militias such as the Irgun and the Stern Gang carried out attacks on Arab communities. The most notorious, Deir Yassin, saw more than 100 civilians murdered. These actions were framed as part of the birth of a nation. I have detailed this extensively in my book *The Rise and Fall of Zionism in the 21st Century*.

Decades later, the perpetrators are memorialised in Israeli street names and museums. Some went on to become prime ministers. The victims, meanwhile, remain stateless, displaced and blamed for their own suffering.

No terrorism label was ever applied. Why?

Because the winners wrote the story.

And once a story is entrenched, once it becomes canon, it is nearly impossible to dislodge. Schoolbooks omit the massacres. Museums erase the victims. Politicians wrap the flag around the perpetrators. And generations grow up believing that state violence is always noble, always necessary and always right.

This is historical amnesia. It allows us to mourn 9/11 but forget Fallujah.
To grieve 7 October but ignore the decades of occupation and dispossession that preceded it.

To condemn the hostage taking of Israelis while treating the siege of Gaza as routine.

In doing so, we create a world where only some lives are sacred, where only some violence is illegitimate, where only the stateless are labelled terrorists, even when their suffering far outweighs their crimes.

And when history forgets the violence of the state, it allows it to happen again.

If the Wounded Knee Massacre is still adorned with medals, how can we say we have learned?

If My Lai fades into footnotes, how can we claim moral leadership?

If every act of terror by a powerful state is renamed, excused or erased, then what exactly do we mean by terrorism?

And who gets to decide?

# CHAPTER THREE

## Section 1: - The Law of Convenience

Terrorism is supposed to be a crime of the gravest kind, an act that endangers the public, strikes fear into civilians and seeks political ends through violence. Yet, for all its supposed clarity, we have seen that terrorism has no single, universal legal definition. There is no common legal thread between nations, no global standard and no agreed line that divides resistance from terror, crime from conflict or protest from insurrection. What we have instead is a patchwork, one stitched together by power rather than principle.

The United Nations illustrates this perfectly. Despite decades of negotiation, the UN has never managed to produce a universally accepted definition of terrorism. Why? Because for every member state, the stakes are political. If terrorism were to be defined too broadly, states might find their own actions falling under the spotlight. If it were defined too narrowly, they might lose the flexibility to target groups they find inconvenient. So, the matter has remained deliberately unresolved.

Into that vacuum, national governments have rushed. Each has constructed its own definition of terrorism, tailored to suit domestic interests and geopolitical agendas. In the United States, the Patriot Act of 2001 cast a sweeping net, allowing almost any politically motivated act of violence, or even preparation for one, to be deemed terrorism. In the UK, terrorism law has been repeatedly expanded to include not only acts of violence but also "glorification," "support" or even "association" with those accused. Under these terms, a person can be prosecuted not for what they have done, but for who they are connected to, or for what they failed to condemn loudly enough.

What starts as law becomes narrative. What begins as legal language quickly becomes a script, one that governments use to tell a story in which they are always the protectors and their enemies are always the threat. In this story, inconvenient opposition can be branded dangerous. Peaceful protest can be watched and monitored. Entire communities, particularly racial, religious or ethnic minorities, can be placed under suspicion without ever having done anything wrong.

This is the danger of the terrorism label written into law: it is not merely a legal tool but a weapon of perception. It allows states to criminalise dissent without calling it censorship, to target communities without calling it racism and to crush political resistance while claiming to uphold public safety.

The law, in this context, does not serve justice. It serves convenience. And that convenience always runs in one direction, towards power.

## Section 2: - The Politics of Designation

The legal designation of a group as "terrorist" is not merely a procedural matter. It is a political act. It unlocks state powers, freezes assets, permits surveillance, allows for arrest without trial and strips away the political legitimacy of any cause that group may represent. Once the label is applied, the conversation effectively ends. The group is no longer a political actor, but a security threat. No longer a resistance, but a danger. No longer someone to talk to, only someone to kill or contain.

But how is this designation made? And by whom?

The answer lies in politics. Across the world, governments have compiled lists of "proscribed" organisations, those labelled as terrorist. These lists vary wildly from country to country. An organisation considered a legitimate political party in one jurisdiction may be banned as a terror group in another. The Kurdish PKK is one such example, labelled terrorist by Turkey, the EU and the U.S., but defended by some human rights groups and left-wing parties across Europe as a resistance movement against oppression. Hezbollah's political and military wings are split in designation, terrorist in the U.S. and UK, but part of Lebanon's democratic process.

Hamas is considered a governing authority by much of the Palestinian population, but a terrorist organisation by Israel and its allies.

These inconsistencies are not anomalies. They are by design. They allow states to tailor the list of enemies according to their foreign policy goals. They reflect not objective threat assessments, but political alignment. A state will call its friends "freedom fighters" and its enemies "terrorists," regardless of method. The label follows the relationship, not the act.

This has deep implications. First, it undermines any pretence that terrorism designations are impartial. Second, it reveals the weaponisation of language as a tool of international diplomacy. Third, it reinforces the idea that legality does not equal morality. A group might act in self-defence, but if they are on the wrong side of geopolitical alliances, their actions will never be considered lawful.

There is no better example of this than the refusal to label state actors themselves as terrorist, no matter the scale of their violence. When Israel launches bombing campaigns in Gaza that result in hundreds of civilian deaths, the terminology is "military response" or "legitimate self-defence." When a Palestinian group retaliates with far less sophisticated means, the response is immediate: "terrorist attack." The difference is not in the action, it is in who gets to define it.

Governments, through selective designation, grant themselves the moral high ground. They write the laws that exempt themselves from accountability, while criminalising those who resist. We have seen this in the UK's designation of Palestine Action as a 'terrorist' grouping. In doing so, they preserve the illusion of legitimacy, even as they commit acts that mirror, or surpass, those of the groups they condemn.

The designation process is not merely flawed. It is corruptible by intent. And it tells us that terrorism, as a legal category, is not about the act. It is about the actor. Or, more precisely, it is about whether the actor is on our side.

## Section 3: - Censorship by Classification

Censorship in the name of security is not new. But in the post-9/11 world, it has taken on new, more insidious forms, especially when it comes to the politics of terrorism. Now, information is not just redacted, it is classified. Not just withheld, but buried. And the justification is almost always the same: national security. Preventing terrorism. Protecting the public.

But what happens when "counterterrorism" becomes a convenient shield to silence dissent, suppress truth, or conceal state wrongdoing?

In the United States, the 2001 Patriot Act fundamentally changed the relationship between citizens and the state. It expanded the surveillance capabilities of the federal government, allowing warrantless wiretaps, indefinite detention, and the monitoring of political and religious groups, all under the justification of terrorism prevention. Whistleblowers who tried to expose abuses, like Edward Snowden, were themselves criminalised. The act became a tool not only for countering threats, but for defining who gets to ask questions and who gets punished for asking.

In the UK, the Terrorism Acts of 2000 and 2006 went even further. They granted sweeping powers to the government to ban organisations, freeze assets, and detain individuals without trial. They also introduced offences like "encouragement of terrorism" and "glorification of terrorism," vague terms that allowed authorities to arrest people for speech, art, or association. One could be labelled a sympathiser simply for liking the wrong post online, quoting a song lyric, or sharing an article.

Consider the 2023 case of a 91-year-old woman in London, arrested during a peaceful demonstration for holding a sign in support of Gaza. She was charged under the UK's terrorism laws for "expressing support for a proscribed organisation." The image of police dragging an elderly pacifist into a van should have caused outrage, but it did not. Because once the word "terrorism" enters the frame, the rules change. Public sympathy diminishes. Due process is suspended. The conversation ends.

In Israel, journalists and human rights organisations have long documented systemic efforts to suppress information about military operations in Gaza and the West Bank. Al Jazeera journalists were repeatedly harassed and, in some cases, killed. NGOs like B'Tselem and Breaking the Silence have been targeted by government officials and accused of treason or terrorism simply for exposing abuses. Netanyahu himself has said that "the terrorists hide behind human rights groups." The goal is clear: equate criticism with danger. Make truth sound like a threat.

The same tactics are used around the world. In India, Kashmir journalists are routinely jailed under anti-terrorism laws for reporting on security crackdowns. In Egypt, counter-terrorism legislation has been used to silence opposition politicians, journalists, and protesters. In Turkey, the government has closed hundreds of media outlets under the justification of fighting terrorism and imprisoned more journalists than almost any country on earth.

In each of these cases, censorship does not wear the old badge of authoritarianism. It wears a new one: "security." And yet the effect is the same. When states control the narrative by criminalising dissent as terrorism, they do not just silence individuals, they reshape public perception.

It is not just information that is hidden. It is perspective. Context. Humanity.

Censorship by classification does not only keep secrets from the public, it keeps morality at bay. When atrocities are hidden, they cannot be condemned. When dissent is criminalised, it cannot build momentum. When victims are labelled as threats, they no longer have rights.

The question we must ask is not whether the state has the right to keep secrets, but what it chooses to hide behind the word terrorism.

Because increasingly, that word is not being used to protect democracy, but to erode it.

## Section 4: - The Silencing Effect

Once the word "terrorist" enters the conversation, everything changes. Rights evaporate. Presumptions of innocence disappear. Sympathy shrinks. And those trying to speak out on behalf of themselves, their families, or their people are suddenly cast not as victims, but as threats.

This is the silencing effect. It works not just on those directly targeted, but on entire communities. It sends a message: speak up, and you too might be labelled. Protest, and your name could land on a watchlist. Organise, and you may find yourself under surveillance. Even if your cause is peaceful. Even if your methods are democratic.

In the UK, Muslims have long warned that counter-terrorism policies like Prevent have created a climate of fear. Teachers are asked to report students for signs of "radicalisation," which can include expressing political views, wearing religious clothing, or criticising Western foreign policy. The line between belief and threat becomes so blurred that Muslim pupils grow up monitored, mistrusted, and muted. Parents tell their children not to talk about

Palestine, Afghanistan, or Islam at school, not because they are ashamed, but because they are afraid.

In the United States, the same silencing extends to Black and progressive activists. When Donald Trump labelled Black Lives Matter a "terrorist movement," he was not just attacking protestors, he was sending a message to every young activist who might take to the streets: we see you as the enemy. ANTIFA too was branded as a domestic terror threat, despite the lack of evidence it exists as a structured group. Once the label was applied, it did not matter. Protestors became suspects. Dissent became dangerous. And the broader public, flooded with images of chaos and crime, began to accept the suppression as necessary.

This is not about isolated rhetoric, it is a strategy. One echoed by authoritarian regimes and illiberal democracies alike. Label dissent as terrorism, and you gain a free pass to ignore, arrest, or even eliminate it. You do not have to listen. You certainly do not have to negotiate. And if the world asks questions, you invoke the magic word: security.

Even religious figures are not safe. In recent years, elderly nuns, priests, and even a 91-year-old pastor have been arrested in Europe and the United States for protesting war, nuclear weapons, or Israeli occupation. Peaceful. Lawful. Moral. But labelled nonetheless as supporting terrorism. Their crime? Association. Their sentence? Public silence.

The silencing effect also works upstream, in the media, in academia, in politics. Writers and commentators who express sympathy for "the wrong side" are blacklisted. Academics who speak about colonialism or resistance find their funding pulled. Politicians who criticise allies are branded as traitors, or worse, apologists for terror. Even UN agencies are not immune: when Israel accused UNRWA of being infiltrated by Hamas, major Western governments cut funding based on unproven claims. An entire humanitarian agency was defunded by accusation.

Guilt by association becomes a blunt tool to mute debate. Even to ask, "why did this happen?" becomes taboo, seen as justification or support. But without understanding context, we cannot hope to solve conflict. Without dialogue, there is only suppression. And with suppression, resentment festers.

The silencing effect does not just punish voices, it poisons discourse. It teaches us not to ask questions, not to look too closely, not to care too deeply. Because caring might put you in the wrong category.

We are told that democracies defend free speech. That ideas must be challenged, not criminalised. And yet, terrorism laws have been stretched so far that they now threaten the very freedoms they claim to protect.

To criticise is not to sympathise. To question is not to betray. But in the age of the terrorism label, nuance is the first casualty.

## Section 5: - When the Law Becomes the Weapon

In theory, the law is blind. It weighs evidence, protects rights, and offers justice without fear or favour. But in the world of counter-terrorism, the law is often anything but impartial. It has become a weapon, deployed not to prosecute violent actors, but to neutralise political threats. And the target is usually whoever stands in the way of state power.

This is not a conspiracy theory. It is a pattern, one that plays out across democracies and dictatorships alike. It always starts the same way: with the expansion of definitions.

Take the word "terrorism" itself. In many legal systems, its meaning has swollen beyond recognition. It no longer refers strictly to politically motivated violence targeting civilians. Instead, it can mean interfering with critical infrastructure, disrupting business, or "threatening public order." In other words: protest. Civil disobedience. Even tweets.

In the UK, the Terrorism Act 2000 gave police sweeping powers to stop, search, and detain people without suspicion. It introduced the concept of "glorification of terrorism," a vague and subjective offence that can criminalise speech, songs, slogans, or symbols. Palestinian flags. Republican murals. Anti-imperialist literature. All open to reinterpretation, depending on who holds power.

In the United States, the Patriot Act, passed in the wake of 9/11, allowed the federal government to detain non-citizens indefinitely without charge, to conduct warrantless surveillance, and to define domestic terrorism so broadly that it includes acts of civil protest. Muslim charities, community organisers, and anti-war activists were among the first casualties. The goal was not just justice, it was intimidation.

But it is not just Anglo-American democracies. India's Unlawful Activities (Prevention) Act has been used to arrest students, journalists, and human rights lawyers under terrorism charges. Israel's anti-terror laws allow indefinite detention without trial for Palestinians. In Turkey, entire Kurdish political parties have been branded as terrorist entities and banned from standing in elections.

When governments are allowed to define terrorism at will, the law stops protecting the people, it starts protecting power.

Even in countries with constitutional protections, legal sleight-of-hand allows states to criminalise opposition. Emergency laws. Special tribunals. National security exceptions. All presented as temporary but often renewed indefinitely. The Special Powers Act in Northern Ireland, for example, allowed for internment without trial and set the stage for decades of resentment and rebellion. It was later mirrored in Guantánamo Bay, where detainees, many never charged, languished for years in legal limbo.

We are now at a stage where the most dangerous thing in the fight against terrorism may be the laws created to fight it. They are overbroad. Under-scrutinised. Politically selective. And disproportionately used against minorities, migrants, and dissenters.

The irony is glaring: those who break the law for political reasons are called terrorists. But those who bend the law to serve political power are called leaders.

This distortion of legality erodes trust, not just in the state, but in the entire justice system. When people see peaceful campaigners jailed, but war criminals walk free, they understand that the law is not neutral. When Netanyahu is accused of war crimes for the starvation and bombardment of Gaza, deemed genocide by some, yet still escapes the terrorism label, while teenagers protesting for Palestine are arrested under terror legislation, the hypocrisy becomes impossible to ignore.

Terrorism law, once a tool of last resort, has become the go-to method for controlling populations. Each time it is abused, it chips away at the moral legitimacy of the state.

The great lie is that this is done for security. The greater truth is that it is done for control.

## Section 6: - The Courts of Exception

Justice, in its truest form, is supposed to be consistent. The same rules for all, the same standards, the same rights. But in the world of terrorism prosecutions, that ideal crumbles. In its place, we find what can only be called "courts of exception," parallel legal universes where normal protections no longer apply.

The logic is simple and seductive: terrorism is a unique threat, so it requires unique measures. But the consequences are far more dangerous than the threat they claim to address. Because once the state creates exceptions to justice, it begins to erode justice itself.

In the United States, the most notorious example is Guantánamo Bay. A legal black hole where the usual rights of the accused—right to a fair trial, right to see evidence, right to legal representation— were suspended. In its prime, the facility held nearly 800 detainees. Many were never charged. Some were children. Others were eventually released without explanation after years of isolation, humiliation, and torture.

The justification? These were "unlawful combatants," not prisoners of war. So international law did not apply. Nor did the Constitution. It was a new category of human, neither citizen nor enemy soldier, just someone stripped of rights because the state said so.

This was not justice. It was convenience masquerading as necessity.

And Guantánamo was not alone. Across the world, governments created their own exceptions. In India, "fast-track courts" for terrorism suspects often deny basic evidentiary standards. In Egypt, thousands of opposition figures and journalists have been tried in mass proceedings, sometimes hundreds at a time, without individual consideration of evidence. In Israel, Palestinian detainees are often subjected to administrative detention, held for months, even years, without charge or trial.

Each of these mechanisms shares a common feature: they bypass the usual rules in the name of urgency.

But these shortcuts rarely catch the masterminds of violence. Instead, they sweep up the vulnerable: the wrongly accused, the politically inconvenient, the marginalised. And they create a chilling effect on society. If your politics or identity places you even adjacent to suspicion, the message is clear: justice does not protect you, it threatens you.

And sometimes, even where due process exists on paper, it is subverted in practice.

Consider the UK's Special Immigration Appeals Commission (SIAC). Here, national security cases are heard using secret evidence. The accused and their lawyers may never be shown the full case against them. Instead, a "special advocate" is appointed, someone who cannot share details with the defendant. It is a theatre of justice, not the real thing. And it raises a fundamental question: can there be a fair trial if the defence is denied the tools to defend?

Or take Control Orders, later replaced by TPIMs (Terrorism Prevention and Investigation Measures), which place individuals under curfew, surveillance, travel bans, and association restrictions without ever charging them with a crime. You do not have to be guilty, just suspected. And you do not get to clear your name, just endure the punishment.

These legal mechanisms serve a powerful narrative: that the threat is too great for the usual rules to apply. But what they really reveal is fear. Not just of terrorism, but of open justice, of transparency, of accountability.

Because once a government believes it cannot win the argument in a fair court, it builds a new court that guarantees the result. The problem with exception is that it rarely stays exceptional. Powers introduced for terrorism seep into ordinary policing, immigration control, and civil society. We saw it during COVID. We see it in climate protest bans. We see it in the surveillance of journalists and lawyers.

If terrorism becomes a magic word that suspends justice, then justice becomes conditional. And that is not justice at all.

## Section 7: - International Hypocrisy and the Two Systems of Law

When it comes to the global war on terrorism, one thing is consistent: inconsistency. The international community often proclaims a commitment to the rule of law, human rights, and the fight against terror. But those values are applied unevenly, selectively enforced depending on who is committing the act and who gets to do the naming.

We live in a world of two legal systems: one for the powerful, and one for everyone else.

Take, for instance, the United Nations Security Council, which regularly condemns "terrorist acts" when committed by non-state actors, particularly in the Global South. Yet when similar violence is carried out by state forces, the language shifts. Aerial bombings that flatten neighbourhoods are labelled "legitimate military operations." Civilians killed in drone strikes are "regrettable collateral damage." And if the perpetrator is a Western ally, the scrutiny often disappears altogether.

Look no further than Israel and Gaza.

When Palestinian militants fire rockets into Israeli towns, it is universally condemned as terrorism. But when Israel launches airstrikes that level entire apartment blocks, kill journalists, or obliterate schools and hospitals, the response is far more muted. Words like "restraint," "self-defence," and "regret" dominate diplomatic statements. Even when entire families are wiped out, the terrorism label is curiously absent.

Consider this paradox: the starvation and systematic killing of civilians in Gaza has been labelled genocide by human rights organisations. Prime Minister Netanyahu is under investigation for war crimes. And yet, the word terrorism is never applied to his government. Why? Is it because he wears a suit? Because he sits at the United Nations? Because terrorism is something that only others do?

Meanwhile, when Palestinians protest or resist, be it through armed resistance, boycotts, or stone-throwing, they are branded not just as violent, but as terrorists. The imbalance could not be starker.

Or take Russia's invasion of Ukraine. The bombardment of civilian infrastructure, forced deportations, and targeting of non-combatants are all textbook definitions of state terror. But the international community reaches for legalese: aggression, war crimes, violations of international law, while avoiding the t-word. Why? Because to call it terrorism might open the door to uncomfortable parallels, like NATO airstrikes in Libya, or U.S. drone campaigns in Yemen and Pakistan.

Even the war in Afghanistan shows this contradiction. When the Taliban attacked U.S. troops, they were terrorists. But when the U.S. accidentally bombed a wedding, killing dozens of civilians, it was chalked up to a tragic error. The act is the same, unprovoked killing of innocent people, but the identity of the killer determines the moral framing.

International hypocrisy is not just frustrating, it is dangerous. It erodes the credibility of global institutions and fuels resentment. It tells the world that justice is not blind, but biased. That some lives are worth more than others. That some violence is justifiable, and other violence is unforgivable, based solely on who commits it.

This two-tiered system has real consequences. It shapes foreign aid. It influences refugee policies. It determines who gets sanctioned, who gets invaded, and who gets a seat at the table.

And it invites a crucial question: if the rules only apply to some, are they really rules at all?

## Section 8: - The Industry of Fear

Terrorism is not just a political concept, it is an industry. A booming, well-funded, and self-perpetuating system that thrives on fear, exaggeration, and the illusion of imminent threat. The so-called "War on Terror" birthed more than military invasions and legal overreach, it created a permanent economy of suspicion.

This industry is built on contracts, consultants, counter-terrorism units, and surveillance empires. And like any good business, it needs a steady supply of product, in this case, terror. Or more accurately, the perception of it.

Consider the explosion in private security firms post-9/11. Governments outsourced everything, from airport screening to military logistics, pouring billions into a market that profits most when the public is most afraid. Entire departments were created, such as the U.S. Department of Homeland Security, now with a budget of over $100 billion, premised on the notion that terrorism was not a threat to be managed, but a war to be won.

But the war never ends, because once you build a system around fear, that fear must be fed.

The more we fear, the more we accept. Warrantless surveillance. Drone killings. Secret prisons. Laws that let the state detain without trial, spy without cause, and silence dissent as if it were sedition. This is how democracies consent to their own erosion, slowly, quietly, in the name of protection.

And the media helps sell the product.

Every time a would-be attacker is arrested, it becomes a headline. Not because of what happened, but because of what might have happened. Bombs that were not built. Plans that were just fantasies. Arrests made under vague suspicions and reported breathlessly before the facts emerge, if they ever do.

Remember the 2006 case of the "Toronto 18"? A group of mostly teenagers, lured into a sting operation involving an undercover agent who provided the plans, the materials, and the encouragement. Or the countless "terror plots foiled" that turned out to be either entrapment or invention.

Fear sells. It boosts ratings. It justifies funding. It feeds populist leaders who promise "safety" if we only give them more power.

The result is a feedback loop. The more we define terrorism broadly, the more "terrorists" appear. The more terrorists we find, the more funding and force we allocate. The more power we grant the state, the more difficult it becomes to distinguish between real threats and political theatre.

And in the middle of it all are ordinary people, targeted, surveilled, and criminalised not because of what they did, but because of who they are. Muslims. Activists. Refugees. People of colour. People in the wrong place, with the wrong name, at the wrong time.

That is the real currency of the terror industry: fear of the Other. Not fear of actual violence, but of the idea that someone, somewhere, with the wrong flag, faith, or grievance, might someday strike.

It is no coincidence that the term "domestic extremist" now includes climate protestors, trade unionists, and anti-capitalist demonstrators. Or that peaceful gatherings like Black Lives Matter have been labelled "terrorist sympathisers" by elected officials. Or that entire movements like ANTIFA, which is not even a formal organisation, have been framed by political leaders, like Donald Trump, as a shadowy internal enemy.

The fear is never meant to end, because when it ends, so does the funding. So does the control.

So the industry keeps ticking. Cameras go up. Rights go down. And every now and then, a politician stands in front of a podium, wagging a finger, invoking the word that silences all doubt: terrorist.

Even when it is just a protestor. Or a nun. Or a 91-year-old woman demanding justice.

## Section 9: - Conclusion – The Weapon That Cannot Be Defined

Terrorism is a word that carries death in its shadow, and yet, no one can agree on what it means. That is its magic. And its danger.

In courtrooms, in parliaments, in newsrooms, the term is hurled like a grenade, shattering nuance and leaving no space for questions. Once the label is attached, the person, the group, the cause is no longer human. They are threat incarnate. And who negotiates with a threat?

But here is the paradox. If we cannot agree on what terrorism is, how can we be so certain about who the terrorists are?

This chapter has traced the fluidity of the term, how laws write it narrowly, how governments bend it broadly, and how media magnifies its usage without ever demanding precision. It is not a definition; it is a decision. A designation made by the powerful, for the powerful.

We have seen how acts of violence are judged not by what they do, but by who does them. A bomb dropped from a drone is strategic. A bomb hidden in a backpack is terror. A state can starve, occupy, and obliterate, and still call itself moral. A boy throwing a rock is terrorism.

We have watched as democracies, frightened and angry, surrendered their rights for the illusion of security. As journalists parroted press releases instead of questioning official narratives. As entire communities, from Gaza to Minneapolis, were branded suspect, not for their actions, but for their identities.

And in this fog, terrorism has become not a word but a weapon.

A weapon used to silence protest. To criminalise resistance. To excuse surveillance, drone strikes, torture, and indefinite detention. A word that permits the inexcusable, because to call something terror is to place it beyond empathy.

We now live in a world where:

• Priests and protestors are branded as sympathisers.

• Aid agencies like UNRWA are defunded because some of their staff allegedly knew a terrorist.

• A state can commit what experts call genocide in Gaza, starvation, siege, bombardment, and still escape the terrorism label.

• Politicians from the U.S. to South Africa, from Israel to Northern Ireland, declare that "there are no innocents," justifying collective punishment on the grounds of collective guilt.

Terrorism has lost its meaning, or perhaps it never had one. It was never about the act. It was always about control.

So we are left with this: a word that ends conversations it should begin. A term that obscures rather than illuminates. A label so potent, so feared, and so abused that it no longer distinguishes the good from the bad, only the strong from the weak.

And that is the most terrifying thing of all.

# CHAPTER FOUR

## Section 1: - The Author of the Story

In every conflict, in every act of violence, there is more than one story. But only one usually makes it to the front page. Only one version is repeated in press briefings, broadcast in rolling news cycles, and etched into public consciousness. That version, whether it is "freedom under attack" or "order restored," is almost always authored by those with the most power, not the most truth.

*Terrorism* is not merely a label of condemnation. It is a narrative instrument. It rewrites a complex reality into something legible, and more importantly, something punishable. The moment a person or group is called a "terrorist," the world stops asking questions. Motives no longer matter. History is erased. Everything that led to the event—the poverty, the persecution, the political context—vanishes behind the curtain of the word.

That is why the ability to define a violent act as "terrorism" is so politically potent. The state, with its vast media networks, legal machinery, and military power, gets to frame violence on its terms. A drone strike on a wedding becomes "a tragic misfire." A riot in a colonised city is "terrorism in the streets." A blockade that starves thousands is "necessary pressure." The vocabulary is not accidental—it is strategic.

Those who get to narrate the event also get to define its morality. This is the essence of narrative power. It is not just about telling a story; it is about ensuring that your version of the story becomes the truth, even if it is a lie.

In recent decades, narrative power has proven to be just as effective as firepower, sometimes more so. A state can massacre a village, jail thousands, or carpet-bomb a city, and still avoid the terrorist label if it controls the narrative. Control the language, and you control the law. Control the images, and you shape the memory.

It is worth asking: how many "terrorists" in today's headlines were never allowed to be anything else?

## Section 2: - Media as Amplifier, Judge, and Jury

If the state authors the story, the media publishes it. Often uncritically. Sometimes enthusiastically. In the war of narratives, the press is not a neutral observer. It is the loudspeaker, the amplification system, the judge and jury that delivers the verdict before a single fact is verified.

In theory, journalism is about truth-seeking, balance, and scrutiny. In practice, particularly in moments of violence, it is about speed, spectacle, and allegiance. When a bomb goes off in a capital city or a plane crashes into a building, the media does not wait. It reacts. In that reaction, it often repeats official language without question. "Suspected terrorist attack." "Extremist ideology." "Islamist militants." These phrases appear within minutes of the incident, not because they have been confirmed, but because they have been assumed.

This instinct to echo authority is especially powerful in times of crisis. Fear is fertile ground for propaganda, and the press, like the public, is susceptible to panic. The problem is that once a story has been framed a certain way, it is almost impossible to reframe it later. The first narrative becomes the dominant one. Rebuttals arrive too late and reach too few.

It is not just about speed; it is about incentives. News outlets rely on clicks, ratings, and attention. Nothing captures attention like terrorism. The word triggers primal emotions: fear, anger, revenge. Editors know this. So do governments. There is a symbiotic relationship: states supply the framing, and media outlets turn it into marketable drama.

Even language reveals bias. When Western soldiers kill civilians, it is called "collateral damage." When a non-state actor kills civilians, it is "terrorism." When an airstrike kills children, it is a "tragic error." When a suicide bomber does the same, it is "barbarism." The outcome is identical. Only the storyteller has changed.

One recent study analysed the New York Times' coverage of different perpetrators of violence. Muslim attackers were 357% more likely to be described using the word "terrorist" than white attackers, even when the acts were comparable. This is not coincidence; it is conditioning. It shapes how entire populations are perceived, profiled, and punished.

The media does not just report on terrorism. It constructs it.

## Section 3: - Manufactured Consent and the Terrorism Narrative

In 1988, Edward S. Herman and Noam Chomsky introduced the concept of *manufacturing consent*, the process by which mass media shape public opinion to align with elite interests. Nowhere is this more evident than in the narrative of terrorism. Governments need the public to believe in the threat. The media help make it real.

Manufactured consent is not about outright lies. It is about framing. It is about what gets highlighted, what gets buried, and what never gets reported at all. When a Western power drops bombs on a wedding party, coverage often focuses on the "intended target" and the "regretful tone" of the spokesperson. When a militant group retaliates, the coverage centres on the carnage, the ideology, the evil. Context disappears. History vanishes. Only the state remains rational. Only the state gets to be sorry.

The terrorism narrative functions like a template. Acts of violence are slotted into a pre-written script depending on the identity of the actor. If the perpetrator is Muslim, the act is quickly linked to a global ideological threat: Islamism, radicalisation, jihad. If the attacker is white, Christian, or affiliated with far-right beliefs, mental illness is often cited first: "lone wolf," "isolated incident," "troubled past." The crime becomes a tragedy, not a threat to national security.

This discrepancy is not just racist. It is strategic. It allows governments to justify military action abroad and repressive policies at home. Surveillance. Detention without trial. Censorship. Border controls. All of it becomes palatable when the threat is presented as existential and external.

The most dangerous element of manufactured consent is its invisibility. People believe they are forming independent opinions when, in fact, they are responding to repeated narratives. The same words. The same images. The same heroes and villains. Over time, the framing becomes so dominant that alternative perspectives are dismissed as fringe, dangerous, or "sympathetic to terrorists."

It also silences the victims. Palestinian mothers, Afghan villagers, Yemeni schoolchildren. When they die at the hands of a drone or an embargo, their stories are rarely told in full. They become statistics: unnamed, unmourned. Because acknowledging their humanity would complicate the narrative. It would remind us that terrorism is not a threat from "over there." It is a label that hides the terror we inflict ourselves.

Manufactured consent ensures that we do not ask the wrong questions, that we do not wonder why some lives matter more than others, and that we do not look too closely at what is done in our name.

## Section 4: - The Platforms and the Panic

There was a time when the state and the press controlled the full narrative. Now, with the rise of digital platforms, that monopoly has fractured but not disappeared. Social media, hailed at first as a tool of liberation, has become just as capable of suppressing dissent and spreading state-approved messaging as traditional outlets. The panic that followed its rise was not about lies. It was about loss of control.

In the aftermath of the Arab Spring, when social media was credited with helping to mobilise revolutions, Western leaders praised it as a force for freedom. But when those same tools began giving voice to marginalised groups in the West—Palestinians, Black Lives Matter protesters, anti-war activists—the mood shifted. Suddenly, platforms were called dangerous, unregulated, and susceptible to "terrorist propaganda."

And so began the clampdown: algorithmic censorship, content takedowns, shadow bans. Tech companies became arbiters of truth but often with a thumb on the scale. Posts that challenged dominant narratives—on Gaza, Yemen, or American drone strikes—were labelled as misinformation or extremist content. Meanwhile, videos glorifying state violence remained online, unquestioned.

The platforms did not create the bias. They inherited it.

Artificial intelligence and content moderation tools reflect the assumptions of those who program them. If the system is trained to flag "terror-related content" using state-sanctioned definitions, then it will suppress Palestinian resistance videos but allow images of U.S. airstrikes. It will mute those calling for accountability while amplifying those demanding retaliation.

This digital asymmetry mirrors the real-world one. In Gaza, during Israel's 2023–2024 bombardment, civilians turned to social media to share their stories, plead for help, and document war crimes. Many saw their accounts suspended or their posts deleted. Platforms said it was due to graphic content. But the same platforms routinely allow violent footage from Western military operations, framed as valiant or necessary, to circulate unchecked.

What emerges is not a free digital square but a moderated battlefield. A place where narratives compete, but some are already disqualified. Where language is policed not by truth but by geopolitics. Where you are more likely to be banned for criticising a war than for starting one.

We are told the internet democratised speech. But in the realm of terrorism, it often just moved the censorship from the newsroom to the algorithm.

## Section 5: - Who Gets the Microphone?

The fight over who gets to speak is the fight over who gets to define reality. In the world of terrorism narratives, that microphone is rarely in the hands of the accused. It is clutched tightly by states, legacy media, and think tanks aligned with power. Victims speak only if their pain fits the official story. Others remain voiceless or, worse, demonised.

When a Western city is attacked, we know the names of every victim within hours. Their stories are told with tenderness. Their lives are honoured. Their communities are offered empathy and aid. But when an airstrike levels a Yemeni wedding, or a Palestinian family is pulled from the rubble in Rafah, there are no tearful profiles. No candlelight vigils. No rolling news coverage. Often, not even names.

The microphone does not just amplify. It selects. It chooses whose grief matters.

In 2023, after a deadly bombing in Gaza that killed over 40 civilians, including children, Israel claimed the target was a Hamas commander. Western media largely echoed the statement without independent verification. The New York Times called it a "precision strike," while the BBC hedged with "Israel says." Few questioned the intelligence behind the claim. Fewer still followed up when it emerged the target may not have even been present. The dead were reduced to context, not content.

Contrast that with attacks on Western soil. The scrutiny is minute. Motives are explored. Backgrounds are investigated. Even the perpetrators are often humanised. Think of the sympathetic coverage of white nationalist shooters, described as "lone wolves," "mentally disturbed," or "misunderstood." The language is careful. The implications are political.

The imbalance is not just in media. It runs through international forums, academic panels, and even funding bodies. Events about "terrorism" rarely feature voices from the regions most bombed or occupied. Palestinian scholars, Afghan journalists, and Yemeni doctors are rarely invited to speak about terrorism, not because they have nothing to say but because their perspective would upend the dominant framing.

This erasure is not accidental. It is strategic. To maintain the illusion that terrorism is something "they" do to "us," the victims of Western and allied violence must remain abstract. Without faces. Without voices. Without microphones.

As journalist Mehdi Hasan once put it, "The media doesn't have a liberal bias. It has a power bias." That bias decides who gets heard. And in the war on terror, silence can be as political as speech.

## Section 6: - Manufactured Consent in the War on Terror

In the wake of 9/11, the world changed, but not only through law or military might. It changed through language, repetition, and the steady manufacture of public consent. George W. Bush did not just declare a "War on Terror"; he made it sound necessary, inevitable, and righteous. The media fell into step. So did most of the public. What followed was not just a war on violent extremists; it was a war on ambiguity, a war on nuance, a war on doubt.

This was not new. The term "manufactured consent" was coined by Walter Lippmann in the 1920s and later expanded by Noam Chomsky and Edward S. Herman to describe how media systems in liberal democracies often serve the interests of elite power. In their model, news is not propaganda in the crude sense; it is filtered. Complex stories are simplified. Outliers are ignored. Dissent is framed as radical or dangerous. What remains is a version of reality that feels neutral, objective, and obvious.

Nowhere was this more evident than in the lead-up to the Iraq War.

The Bush administration repeatedly linked Saddam Hussein to al-Qaeda, despite no evidence of operational ties. They claimed Iraq possessed weapons of mass destruction. These claims were broadcast across every major network. "We don't want the smoking gun to be a mushroom cloud," warned then-National Security Advisor Condoleezza Rice. The phrase was repeated hundreds of times. The drums of war were beaten not by soldiers but by news anchors.

By the time it became clear there were no WMDs, the war was well underway. Over 100,000 Iraqi civilians were dead. Hundreds of thousands more were displaced. But by then, the narrative had moved on.

Manufactured consent does not require lies. It only requires repetition and the omission of inconvenient truths. It works through framing: if terrorism is always something "they" do, then "we" are always responding, never provoking. If our bombs are smart and their bombs are cowardly, then our violence is virtuous and theirs is vile. Consent for war is manufactured not by proving necessity but by making opposition unthinkable.

This consent extends to domestic policy too. Laws like the USA PATRIOT Act or the UK's Prevent strategy were passed with minimal public resistance, in part because the media framed them as safety measures. Critics were dismissed as naïve or unpatriotic. The binary was established: you are either with us or with the terrorists.

And when consent is finally challenged, when whistleblowers, journalists, or civil society voices try to interrupt the narrative, they are often labelled as dangerous themselves. Edward Snowden did not just leak information about illegal surveillance; he was branded a traitor. Julian Assange, who published war crimes, became a cautionary tale. The message is clear: challenge the consensus and you might find yourself on the wrong side of the microphone and the law.

In this environment, terrorism becomes not just a threat but a justification for war, for censorship, for surveillance, and for the silencing of dissent. Consent is not gathered. It is produced. Engineered. Manufactured.

## Section 7: - The Narrative of the Heroic State

Every nation tells stories about itself: founding myths, noble sacrifices, moments of peril and triumph. But for powerful states, especially those engaged in perpetual war, these stories become something more. They evolve into shields, into scripts, into armour against accountability.

The modern state does not simply wield power; it must justify it. And so, narratives are crafted in which the state is always the reluctant actor, the principled force, the defender of order against chaos. These are not lies in the traditional sense. They are curated truths: selective, framed, stylised. And through repetition, they become doctrine.

America is perhaps the clearest example. From the Revolution to the War on Terror, U.S. foreign policy has been framed as a series of moral interventions: liberating the oppressed, defending freedom, restoring peace. Even when the record shows otherwise—Vietnam, Iraq, drone wars in Yemen and Somalia—the story persists. The script does not change. We are the good guys.

Barack Obama, a Nobel Peace Prize laureate, personally authorised hundreds of drone strikes, many resulting in civilian deaths. Yet his narrative remained intact: precision warfare, surgical strikes, moral calculus. Few Western media outlets questioned the premise. After all, the storyteller was polished, articulate, presidential. In the heroic state narrative, appearances matter as much as outcomes.

Israel, too, frames itself as eternally besieged, surrounded by threats, forced to defend its citizens. Its military operations in Gaza are described as "mowing the lawn," a clinical, almost agricultural metaphor for recurring bombardments. Civilian casualties are labelled unfortunate, inevitable, or a result of Hamas "using human shields." Rarely is the assumption challenged that one side alone is entitled to self-defence. The heroic state, by definition, cannot be a terrorist.

This framing has global consequences. If the state is always the hero, then those who oppose it must be villains. Protesters become agitators. Whistleblowers become traitors. Entire communities— Muslims in the West, Palestinians in Gaza, Black activists in the U.S.—are cast as suspect populations. The state, meanwhile, claims the moral high ground even while deploying violence, surveillance, and coercion.

This is not limited to democracies. Authoritarian regimes also exploit the heroic state narrative. Vladimir Putin describes Russia's invasion of Ukraine as a "special military operation" to liberate Russian speakers. China justifies its Uyghur re-education camps as counter-extremism and poverty alleviation. The script is adapted, but the structure remains: the state is never wrong. It is never violent. It is never the terrorist.

The danger is not only that these narratives are false, but that they are totalising. Once established, they absorb all contradiction.

Victims become collateral. Critics become enemies. In the end, justice becomes whatever the state says it is.

History remembers differently. The same America that justified its war in Vietnam with talk of domino theory and democracy left behind three million dead Vietnamese and an enduring legacy of trauma. The same Britain that declared peacekeeping in Kenya committed atrocities in Mau Mau detention camps. The gap between the narrative and reality is vast, but the narrative is what lives on in textbooks, speeches, and political memory.

The heroic state tells us that violence is sometimes necessary, that it is unfortunate but justified. But what if the hero is unreliable? What if the storyteller is the real source of the danger?

## Section 8: - Silencing the Other Story

If the state controls the dominant narrative, then what becomes of the voices that challenge it? The answer, too often, is silence, not through absence but through erasure, distortion, and criminalisation.

Every story has a counter-story. Every bombed city has a testimony. Every "precision strike" has survivors. But these alternative truths rarely make it past the barriers of media framing, official briefings, and national myth-making. When they do, they are met with suspicion, delegitimisation, or outright repression. The truth is not denied; it is simply buried beneath noise.

Consider the case of Al Jazeera journalist Shireen Abu Akleh, shot in the head while reporting in the West Bank in 2022. Despite eyewitness accounts, video footage, and independent investigations pointing to Israeli forces as responsible, the dominant media narrative hesitated, hedged, and equivocated. Phrases like "crossfire" and "unconfirmed" were deployed to create ambiguity where there was clarity. The power to tell the story overpowered the story itself.

Silencing the other story takes many forms. In occupied Palestine, it is the bombing of press offices. In Russia, it is the jailing of dissident journalists. In the United States, it is the use of the Espionage Act against whistleblowers like Edward Snowden. In India, it is the arrest of student leaders and human rights defenders accused of "sedition" or "terror links." The pattern is global. The state, no matter how democratic in name, cannot tolerate narratives that expose its violence, contradictions, or hypocrisies.

Language is a key tool in this silencing. Protesters become "rioters." Resistance becomes "instigation." Civil disobedience becomes "terrorist sympathy." In the UK, Palestine Action protesters, some of them priests, elderly nuns, even a 91-year-old woman, were arrested under terrorism-related charges for peaceful direct action. Their crime was targeting weapons manufacturers supplying Israel. In the U.S., Donald Trump labelled Black Lives Matter as a "terrorist movement," while his administration lumped Antifa, environmental activists, and anti-fascists into vague "domestic extremism" categories. The purpose of such labels is not clarity; it is control.

This silencing is not merely rhetorical. It shapes law, policy, and public perception. The defunding of UNRWA, the United Nations agency providing humanitarian aid in Gaza, is a stark example. On the basis of unproven Israeli allegations that some staff were linked to Hamas, entire funding streams were withdrawn, crippling the only lifeline for millions. The Palestinian narrative, that they are occupied, besieged, and brutalised, was overwritten by a single accusation of "terrorist association."

In modern conflict, silencing is not achieved by censorship alone. It is achieved by overwhelming the narrative space, by flooding it with official statements, think tank reports, embedded journalists, and media trained to "balance" the unbalanced. A destroyed hospital becomes a "possible command centre." A grieving mother becomes a "Hamas sympathiser." A starvation campaign becomes "logistical pressure." The truth drowns in euphemism.

But the other story is not dead. It lives in exile, in underground publications, in the voices of the displaced, in diaspora networks, in grainy phone footage, and in testimony smuggled through firewalls. It lives in books like this one, in conversations whispered beneath the roar of state propaganda.

The question is not whether the other story exists. The question is whether we are still willing to listen.

# PART II: When the State Is Violent

# CHAPTER FIVE

## Section 1: - The Myth of Clean War

In modern warfare, states have cultivated a narrative that distances their actions from the chaos and brutality of the battlefield. Precision. Intelligence-led. Surgical. These are the buzzwords deployed to reassure the public that when states wage war, they do so cleanly and efficiently. Within this myth lies a dangerous assumption: that state violence is not only justified but refined. That it is measured, controlled, and rational, unlike the chaotic rage of "terrorists."

But the myth of clean war collapses under even mild scrutiny. Civilian casualties, infrastructure obliteration, and environmental devastation are all common features of state-led military campaigns. In reality, modern state warfare is not clean. It is not precise. It is simply better branded.

Take drone warfare, for example. The United States has claimed for years that its drone strikes in countries like Yemen, Pakistan, and Somalia are "targeted," eliminating terrorist threats with minimal collateral damage. Yet independent investigations, including those by The Intercept and Amnesty International, have revealed a more disturbing picture. Drone strikes have killed wedding parties, medical workers, journalists, and children. In one leaked document, U.S. military data revealed that nearly 90 per cent of people killed in drone strikes during a five-month period were not the intended targets.

Still, this is not called terrorism. It is framed as tragic but necessary. The loss of innocent life is absorbed into the broader narrative of defence. "We regret the loss of civilian life," say official statements, "but these actions are essential to keeping our country safe." The statement is never followed by a question: safe from whom, exactly? Because asking that would collapse the logic of the justification.

This one-sided moral economy, where the deaths of innocents are acceptable if caused by the state, stands in stark contrast to how violence by non-state actors is portrayed. A bomb set off in a marketplace by a resistance group is terrorism. But a missile dropped on the same marketplace by an F-16 is a strategic miscalculation, an "intelligence failure," or a regrettable but permissible cost of modern war.

When Israel bombs Gaza, collapsing apartment blocks and killing entire families, it invokes the "right to self-defence." When Palestinians fire rockets in retaliation, mostly crude and unguided, it is labelled terrorism. There is no equivalence, no symmetry, and crucially, no equal claim to the right to defend.

In 2021, during a heated international debate over violence in Gaza, Israeli Prime Minister Benjamin Netanyahu was asked in a U.S. interview whether Palestinians had the same right to defend themselves. He replied bluntly: "No." That single word, unexplained and unchallenged, illustrates the deep asymmetry in how rights and legitimacy are distributed in modern geopolitics.

This is not just hypocrisy. It is a carefully maintained hierarchy of violence. State violence is institutionally excused and linguistically sanitised, while resistance violence is framed as existential threat. The state wages war. The terrorist commits atrocities.

This framing has real-world consequences. It determines which lives are grievable and which are not. It shapes foreign policy, public opinion, arms sales, and media coverage. It conditions populations to accept war as peace, occupation as order, and mass death as mere "collateral damage."

The truth is stark. The myth of clean war enables dirty outcomes. It allows states to commit horrors in full view of the international community and to do so with impunity.

## Section 2: - The Right to Defend – For Some

The right to self-defence is one of the most sacred principles in international law. Enshrined in Article 51 of the UN Charter, it grants every nation the legal and moral authority to protect its sovereignty and its citizens. Yet, like many lofty ideals in global politics, the application of this right is anything but equal. Not all states are permitted to defend themselves, and certainly not all peoples.

This selective application is one of the most glaring hypocrisies in the global discourse on terrorism and violence. It is why Israel, for example, is granted a permanent claim to defence, even as it maintains a seventeen-year blockade on Gaza, expands illegal settlements, and is currently accused of perpetrating genocide. Meanwhile, Palestinians, dispossessed, stateless and occupied, are routinely denied that same right. When they resist, they are labelled terrorists. When they protest, they are dismissed as agitators. When they retaliate, they are condemned as barbarians.

The asymmetry was laid bare in a 2021 interview when Prime Minister Benjamin Netanyahu was asked, plainly and directly, whether Palestinians had the right to defend themselves. His answer was, "No." Not couched in legal nuance. Not justified by strategy. Simply a flat denial. A population of over two million in Gaza, half of them children, denied even the theoretical right to resist airstrikes, siege or displacement.

And Netanyahu is not alone. Across Western capitals, from Washington to London, political leaders have parroted the line, "Israel has the right to defend itself." But rarely, if ever, do they complete the sentence: "Palestinians do not." To say it openly would be to admit what has long been the reality: this right is not universal. It is a privilege reserved for allies.

This pattern repeats across the globe. In Ukraine, the West proudly declares support for the Ukrainian people's right to resist invasion, occupation and war crimes. Arms flow freely. Rhetoric is loud. Sanctions are swift. Yet when the victims are brown, stateless or Muslim, the calculation changes. The right to defend becomes conditional, even criminal.

Consider Iraq in 2003. The US-led invasion was framed as pre-emptive self-defence, a war to prevent terrorism. Never mind that Iraq had no weapons of mass destruction. Never mind that over one hundred thousand civilians died. Never mind that the justification unravelled in real time. The narrative of self-defence persisted. It shielded decision-makers from accountability and reframed catastrophic violence as noble.

Meanwhile, when Iraqi militias resisted occupation, when roadside bombs targeted convoys, or when young men took up arms against foreign troops on their own soil, it was called insurgency, or worse, terrorism. One side defended, the other attacked. One side liberated, the other destabilised.

This double standard is not incidental. It is structural. It is how international power operates. To be allowed to defend oneself, one must first be recognised as worthy of rights.

That is the crux of the issue. Defence is not merely an act; it is a status. It is a designation conferred by those with the power to grant legitimacy. It is why the United States can bomb Syria in the name of national security, yet a Syrian response would be condemned as aggression. It is why drone strikes in Somalia are classified as counter-terrorism, while retaliatory attacks by local groups are framed as terror plots.

And it is why Palestinians can be shelled, starved and bombed, yet still be told they do not have the right to fight back.

If the right to defend is recognised only when exercised by the powerful, then it is not a right at all. It is a narrative tool, a justification for violence wrapped in legal language.

In this world, only some people are allowed to survive on their own terms. Others must die quietly or risk being labelled a threat.

## Section 3: - Gaza, Genocide, and the Terrorism That Isn't

There is no modern conflict more emblematic of the hypocrisy surrounding the word *terrorism* than Gaza. A walled-in strip of land, barely twenty-five miles long, home to more than two million Palestinians, half of them children, has become both a laboratory and a graveyard for what state violence looks like when it is reframed as justice. Here, in full view of the world, we have witnessed the slow, deliberate dismantling of a people, bomb by bomb, blockade by blockade, without ever once applying the label that has justified so many lesser acts elsewhere: terrorism.

Instead, the violence in Gaza is constantly recast through a different lens. Israel, the state, has the right to defend. The strikes are *targeted*. The casualties are *collateral*. The intent is *security*. But take a step back, remove the labels, and ask yourself: what do we call it when apartment buildings are flattened with families inside? When hospitals and refugee camps are hit? When water, power, and medicine are cut off from a civilian population? If not terrorism, what?

By October 2023, during the largest Israeli military campaign in Gaza's history, over thirty thousand Palestinians had been killed, the majority of them civilians. More than a third were children. Entire neighbourhoods were levelled. Schools were converted into shelters, then bombed. Ambulances were struck. Journalists were killed. UN officials began to warn, in increasingly urgent terms, of a looming genocide. And still, the word *terrorist* was reserved, not for the state doing the bombing, but for those under the rubble.

This is the Gaza paradox. The population most subjected to systematic violence, displacement, and blockade is also the one most consistently denied the right to resist. When Hamas launches rockets, it is terrorism. When Israel launches two-thousand-pound bombs into residential towers, it is self-defence. The weapon matters less than the wielder, the casualties less than the narrative.

And this narrative is maintained not just by Israel, but by its allies. The United States, the UK, the EU—all rushed to affirm Israel's right to defend itself after the October 7 attacks. They funded, armed, and diplomatically shielded its campaign. Yet not one called the months-long assault on Gaza an act of terror. Even as bodies piled up in schoolyards. Even as hunger and disease spread. Even as UN agencies declared it a humanitarian catastrophe. The label did not apply, not to the state, not to its actions, not even in the face of overwhelming evidence.

In fact, the opposite happened. The United Nations Relief and Works Agency (UNRWA), the main provider of food, health, and education in Gaza, was defunded by key Western states after Israel alleged that a handful of its employees had links to Hamas. No trial. No due process. Guilt by association. Aid was halted for millions based on unproven accusations against a few. The people of Gaza were not just abandoned; they were punished.

This weaponisation of guilt is part of a broader strategy. If you can conflate civilians with terrorists, then you can kill civilians without consequence. If a population is rebranded as complicit, then there are "no innocents." This was made explicit in statements from Israeli officials and Western commentators. Some claimed that Gazans who stayed were human shields. Others suggested that even children could not be considered non-combatants because they had been *indoctrinated*. It is the logic of extermination, and it hides behind the mask of anti-terrorism.

And yet, in the heart of this horror, there are voices of clarity. Israeli journalist Gideon Levy, long a critic of his own government, has written scathingly about what he calls the "divine exemption" granted to Israel. "We are a people for whom international law does not apply," he observed. "God's chosen people are excused from war crimes. Our terror is called defence. Their defence is called terror."

This is not just about Gaza. It is about the precedent we set when we allow powerful states to write their own definitions of violence and to exempt themselves from accountability. It is about the slow erosion of a word that once meant something, and now means whatever the powerful say it means.

Because if the deliberate bombing of schools, ambulances, and aid convoys is not terrorism, then the word has lost all meaning.

## Section 4: - Guilt by Association – The UNRWA Example

If war is the theatre of violence, then narrative is the script, and in that script, the role of villain is easily assigned by association. Nowhere is this more dangerously evident than in the treatment of UNRWA, the United Nations Relief and Works Agency for Palestine Refugees. For decades, UNRWA has been the lifeline for millions of Palestinians, particularly in Gaza, providing food, medical aid, education, and shelter in a place where infrastructure has been shattered repeatedly by war. But in the febrile climate following the October 7 Hamas attacks, the agency itself became a target, not because of what it had done, but because of who it served.

The trigger came in January 2024, when Israel alleged that twelve UNRWA employees had participated in or aided the October 7 attacks. No court case. No cross-examination. No public evidence. And yet, almost immediately, key Western countries including the United States, the UK, Germany, and Canada cut off funding to the organisation, effectively threatening the survival of the only humanitarian structure still functioning inside Gaza at the time.

Twelve people out of over 13,000 staff in Gaza. That is less than 0.1 per cent of the workforce. Even if the allegations were true, and they remain contested, what followed was not justice. It was collective punishment masquerading as due diligence. An entire population was punished for the unproven actions of a dozen people. Food deliveries stopped. Medical supplies dwindled. Water and sanitation services collapsed. Children, the elderly, the wounded, none of them had any connection to those accused, but they were all made to suffer.

This was guilt by association raised to the level of international policy.

UNRWA's suspension is not just a tragedy. It is a signal. It shows that the humanitarian space itself can be delegitimised, defunded, and destroyed if it serves the wrong population. It reveals that even neutrality can be recast as complicity. The very act of helping Palestinians, of treating them as human beings deserving of care, can now be portrayed as supporting terrorism.

This logic is deeply corrosive. It implies that any institution working in Palestinian territories is suspect. That to educate a Palestinian child is to indoctrinate them. That to feed a Palestinian family is to prolong resistance. This dehumanising narrative does not just impact Gaza, it reverberates across international law and humanitarian practice. It poisons the principle of impartiality. And once that is gone, the Geneva Conventions become mere suggestions.

Indeed, the UN's own investigation into Israel's claims concluded that many of the allegations were exaggerated or unsubstantiated. But the damage had already been done. Funding was frozen. Aid convoys halted. And Gaza, already reeling from blockade and bombardment, was plunged deeper into humanitarian catastrophe. This is not a side-effect of war. It is policy by other means.

And consider the hypocrisy. Israel has, for years, faced credible accusations of war crimes, from collective punishment to indiscriminate bombing to the use of white phosphorus. Yet no Western country cut diplomatic ties. No defence pacts were paused. No military aid was suspended. But when a handful of aid workers were accused, without trial, of acting improperly, the entire support system for millions was switched off almost overnight. That is not proportionality. It is narrative management.

In this framework, terrorism is not about the act, or even the intent. It is about affiliation, proximity, geography. A Palestinian mother receiving flour from UNRWA is closer to being labelled complicit in terror than the pilot who dropped the bomb that killed her child.

And that is the real danger. If we start treating entire populations as suspect, then the protections of international law fall away. And when those protections vanish, so too does the line between war and atrocity.

Guilt by association becomes a self-fulfilling prophecy. By branding entire institutions, aid agencies, and communities as tainted, states can justify ever more extreme acts. The label *terrorist* is no longer an accusation, it becomes a weapon, a pretext, a shield against scrutiny.

In the end, the UNRWA episode is not just about Gaza. It is about how the war on terror has morphed into a war on compassion, about how helping the wrong people can make you guilty by default, and about how the world's most vulnerable are now also the most suspect, because they are not just victims of war, but victims of a word.

# CHAPTER SIX

## Section 1: - The Invisible Weapon

War is often imagined as gunfire and explosions, tanks and drones, missiles and blood. But modern warfare has evolved. Today, some of the most devastating tools of violence do not leave craters in the earth. They leave empty shelves, empty stomachs, and hollowed-out economies. Starvation, siege, and sanctions have become the quiet weapons of contemporary statecraft. They kill slowly, often without images to shock the world. They operate in the shadows of legality and morality. And yet, the human cost is no less horrific.

When a state denies food, fuel, medicine, or electricity to an entire population, whether through blockade, embargo, or bureaucratic suffocation, it is engaging in a form of violence that often escapes the label of terrorism. Why? Because it is framed as policy, as necessity, as pressure, as diplomacy. Euphemisms abound: "targeted sanctions," "strategic isolation," "security-based containment." But the outcome is unmistakable: suffering on a mass scale.

Consider Gaza. For years, its 2.3 million residents have lived under an Israeli blockade that controls everything from electricity to the number of calories permitted into the Strip per day. In 2006, an Israeli official referred to it as "putting Palestinians on a diet," a chilling phrase that exposes the cruelty embedded in policy. The siege is justified in the name of security. But what is the distinction between launching a bomb at a bakery and preventing flour from entering a neighbourhood? One is immediate destruction, the other is slow death.

International law is clear. Collective punishment is a war crime. The Geneva Conventions prohibit the starvation of civilians as a method of warfare. And yet, when states do it, especially powerful ones, they often receive not condemnation but complicity. Aid is restricted. Journalists are barred. Bureaucrats and diplomats issue statements that avoid blame. And still, people die.

The use of starvation and siege is not limited to one conflict or one geography. From Yemen to Syria, from Iraq to Venezuela, the tactic is the same: weaken a people by depriving them of the means to live. And it is almost always justified by pointing to the "enemy within": a government, a faction, a group. The suffering of civilians is written off as unfortunate but necessary. A by-product. Collateral. Not the point, but always the price.

So here we must ask: if terrorism is defined by the deliberate targeting of civilians for political ends, what else is this? When a state strangles a population to force political compliance, is that not terror by another name? And if it is, why are those who implement it never called terrorists?

## Section 2: - The Siege Economy – Gaza as a Case Study

Gaza is often spoken of in terms of conflict, of war, of rocket fire and retaliation. But it is also the world's most enduring and deliberately engineered siege. And perhaps the clearest modern example of how starvation, restriction, and isolation can be wielded as weapons, quiet, bureaucratic, deniable weapons, by a state actor with full impunity.

Since 2007, when Hamas took control of the Gaza Strip, Israel has imposed a land, sea, and air blockade, with Egypt enforcing parts of it from the south. This blockade, though officially justified as a security response to prevent weapons smuggling, has evolved into something far more sinister: a system of calibrated economic throttling, intentionally designed to weaken not just Hamas, but the population itself.

The Israeli government has long framed this as a war against a terrorist group. But leaked policy documents and public statements over the years have revealed a different truth. In 2012, an Israeli court forced the government to release a Ministry of Defence document that literally calculated the minimum calorie intake required per person in Gaza to avoid malnutrition, effectively putting a cap on how much food was permitted into the territory. It was not a military strategy. It was siege by spreadsheet.

Add to this the restrictions on construction materials, medicine, fuel, electricity, and even fishing zones, and it becomes clear that the objective is not merely the containment of militants, but the slow suffocation of an entire society. Infrastructure collapses. Hospitals run out of supplies. Electricity is rationed to a few hours a day. Unemployment soars. Children suffer from stunted growth and PTSD before they reach ten.

It is, in every sense, economic warfare. And yet it is not described in such terms by the majority of the Western media or international political class. The term "terrorism" is reserved for the rockets fired outward, not for the calculated strangulation enforced inward. When children die because dialysis machines have no power, it is not called state violence. When clean water is inaccessible and disease spreads, it is not labelled terrorism. It is filed under "humanitarian concern."

And here lies the paradox. Israel is considered a democratic state, a Western ally, and a sovereign nation defending itself. Gaza, by contrast, is depicted as a lawless enclave ruled by terrorists. But which side enforces the policy that deliberately deprives civilians of basic human needs? Which side controls the borders, the airspace, and the sea? Which side holds the power?

Even when reports by UN agencies and human rights organisations declare the siege illegal and inhumane, there are few consequences. Gaza remains under blockade. And Israel remains untouchable in the court of international public opinion.

The suffering of Palestinians is reframed, not as the consequence of policy, but as the fault of their leaders. As if occupation, deprivation, and trauma are somehow deserved. As if a civilian's right to food and medicine is conditional on their government's behaviour.

In no other context would this be accepted. If Russia blockaded Kyiv and starved its residents to force a surrender, it would be called terrorism, or war crimes at minimum. If China cut off electricity and insulin to Taiwan, the world would erupt in condemnation. But when it happens in Gaza, the language shifts. The horror is softened. And the label "terrorist" remains firmly on the shoulders of the besieged, not the besieger.

## Section 3: - Sanctions with Teeth – Economic Violence on a Global Scale

Sanctions are often marketed as a humane alternative to war, non-violent, diplomatic pressure intended to change bad behaviour without shedding blood. But what if that pressure starves children? What if it collapses hospitals, triggers medicine shortages, or destroys livelihoods? At what point do sanctions become something else, less policy, more punishment? Less diplomacy, more economic terrorism?

In theory, sanctions are precise instruments aimed at political elites. In practice, they are blunt tools that almost always strike the most vulnerable first. The logic is simple: make life hard enough for ordinary people, and they will either pressure their government to change course or topple it altogether. But this theory rarely plays out. Instead, authoritarian regimes grow more entrenched, while citizens grow more desperate.

Consider Iran. Decades of U.S. and international sanctions, many intensified under the Trump administration, have devastated its economy. The official line was that sanctions targeted the

Revolutionary Guard and nuclear activities, but the real impact was far wider. Cancer patients could not access essential medication. Air pollution spiked due to a lack of equipment parts. Inflation soared. The Iranian rial collapsed. Children died, not because of military action, but because the international banking system would not process transactions for medicine. When ordinary civilians die slow deaths by economic asphyxiation, where is the moral high ground?

Or Venezuela, where sanctions imposed by the U.S. and others, again aimed at toppling a regime, crippled oil production, slashed public services, and helped fuel a humanitarian catastrophe that forced millions to flee. Former UN Special Rapporteur Alfred de Zayas called these sanctions "economic warfare" and stated unequivocally: "Modern-day economic sanctions and blockades are comparable with medieval sieges of towns with the intention of forcing them to surrender." He added, "Twenty-first century sanctions attempt to bring not just a town, but sovereign countries to their knees."

Sanctions do not explode buildings. They do not send drones into wedding parties or tanks into neighbourhoods. But they do kill. Quietly. Slowly. Without the visuals that provoke outrage. And so, they are rarely framed as violence. Even less often are they framed as terrorism.

But if terrorism is defined, as it so often is, as the use of violence or intimidation against civilians to achieve political goals, then how are sanctions different? They intimidate. They destroy. They cause suffering with the explicit intent of altering political outcomes. The only difference is that they are sanctioned by states, by coalitions, by institutions that assume the moral authority to decide who deserves to be punished and who does not.

And here again, the double standard reveals itself. When Hamas, or Hezbollah, or even leftist insurgents in Latin America use blockades or economic sabotage, they are terrorists. When the

United States or European Union cuts off an entire nation's access to international markets, it is "foreign policy." The intent may be the same. The outcomes can be identical. But the label is determined by who holds the microphone.

This is narrative power at its most insidious. One man's siege is another's policy tool. One country's destruction of civilian life is a necessary evil. Another's terrorism. The acts are similar. The results are often worse. But the moral outrage is selective, and the labels are doled out accordingly.

We live in a world where death by drone is called self-defence, and death by hunger is called economic reform. Where state actors can destroy entire economies in the name of democracy, and face no reckoning for the human toll. Where violence is not judged by its nature, but by its passport.

## Section 4: - The New Front Line – Technology and Digital Blockades

In the 21st century, war has expanded beyond borders, battlefields, and bombs. Today, conflict lives in code, in servers, software, payment systems, and communication networks. And like their physical counterparts, these digital battlegrounds are weaponised by those with power, not just to fight enemies, but to control narratives, isolate populations, and enforce submission without a single soldier crossing a line.

This is the new face of sanctions: the digital blockade.

Think of a nation like Cuba, already reeling from decades of economic isolation, further cut off from global platforms like PayPal, Amazon, or Zoom. Or think of Iran, where international tech restrictions mean universities struggle to access scientific databases, developers cannot use critical open-source tools, and everyday people are locked out of cloud storage and encrypted messaging apps. The goal is clear: choke off progress. Halt connection. Prevent the flow of information that might sustain opposition or fuel autonomy.

But this is not just about denying Netflix to rogue regimes. The digital blockade strikes at something deeper: the infrastructure of modern life. Payment processors. Software updates. Cloud-based services. These are no longer luxuries; they are essentials, just as vital to a country's survival as oil or water. To cut a nation off from these is not a gesture. It is a strike.

And again, the collateral damage is profound. Tech companies routinely comply with government sanctions, even pre-emptively, out of fear of legal or financial penalty. The result: Afghan aid workers locked out of banking apps. Syrian doctors unable to access online medical journals. North Korean defectors abroad unable to communicate with family. Lives disrupted. Development stalled. Dissent silenced. Not by gunfire or bombs, but by login errors and 404 screens.

And yet, we rarely ask whether this too is a form of terrorism.

What do you call it when a state or coalition of states intentionally inflicts suffering on civilians through technological denial? When access to knowledge, tools, communication, and livelihood is systematically cut off in the name of regime change or political leverage? The intent is clear. The target is clear. The suffering is real. But because the violence is intangible, coded in software and enforced by bureaucracy, it escapes the terrorism label entirely.

The same act, carried out by non-state actors, hacking power grids, disrupting hospitals, blocking access to information, would be swiftly labelled cyber-terrorism. But when done by the powerful, it becomes geopolitics, policy, strategy.

And the consequences are obscured.

Even humanitarian organisations are caught in the crossfire. Sanctions and digital restrictions make it harder for them to transfer funds, coordinate operations, and reach vulnerable communities. In some cases, NGOs have withdrawn altogether, not because of direct threats, but because of compliance fears. The weaponisation of regulation has achieved what bullets could not: paralysis.

This is the future of state violence, faceless, quiet, and automated. It does not shock the conscience because it does not bleed. But it inflicts harm just the same. And like all violence committed by states, it is given cover by the rhetoric of security, order, and necessity.

The irony is that as the world becomes more connected, the tools of disconnection have become the most effective weapons. And in this new reality, power is not just about military might. It is about who controls the switch.

Who can shut off the servers.

Who can crash the currency.

Who can silence the signal.

Who decides who gets to speak, and who must disappear into digital darkness.

## Section 5: - Gaza and the Blueprint of Economic Erasure

If starvation is a weapon, Gaza is its test site.

For nearly two decades, the Gaza Strip has existed under a form of siege that most of the world dares not call what it is: an economic war zone. Not declared, not televised in the traditional sense, but relentless and exacting nonetheless. It is a blockade by design, of food, fuel, medicine, construction materials, internet access, electricity, water. A deliberate throttling of life's necessities.

And it is not accidental. It is not the by-product of conflict. It is the strategy.

In 2012, the Israeli government admitted what many had long suspected: it had developed a calorie calculation for Gaza. An actual spreadsheet determining the minimum caloric intake necessary to avoid malnutrition, just enough to prevent a humanitarian catastrophe, but not enough to allow for dignity, autonomy, or growth. That is not a defensive measure. That is a laboratory model for economic erasure.

Israeli journalist Amira Hass described it best: Gaza is not just under occupation, it is under experiment. Every facet of life is managed, surveilled, or restricted, not for security, but for control. And when that control is broken, when protests erupt, rockets fly, or international pressure mounts, the punishment is immediate: bombing raids, power cuts, fuel blockades, and food shortages.

The 2023 to 2025 period has made this clearer than ever.

In the aftermath of October 7, Israel declared an all-out siege on Gaza: "No electricity, no food, no fuel, no water." Not just for Hamas, but for everyone. Aid convoys were blocked. Hospitals ran on fumes. Newborn babies died in incubators without power. Water became undrinkable. Malnutrition skyrocketed. Entire neighbourhoods were reduced to rubble. It was not just war, it was the weaponisation of absence.

And yet, this is not called terrorism. It is called retaliation. Security. A necessary response.

Even though UN experts, legal scholars, and humanitarian observers have warned of collective punishment, a war crime under international law, the dominant narrative persists. It is not terrorism because it is carried out by a state, because the victims are Palestinians, because the perpetrators are seen as Western allies. The terrorism label does not apply.

But ask yourself: if another actor, a militia, a rebel group, a paramilitary force, imposed a siege that starved hundreds of thousands, bombed civilians, shut off aid, and levelled schools and mosques, would we not call it terrorism?

Would we not demand sanctions, tribunals, justice?

Instead, we watch as an entire population is systematically deprived, and the language of international diplomacy ties itself in knots to avoid stating the obvious.

Gaza is the blueprint. It has shown the world that economic erasure can be deployed as policy without triggering global outrage, so long as you control the narrative, so long as you are not labelled the terrorist.

And in this silence, new frontlines are born. Other regimes watch. Other sieges are planned. Other populations are punished.

The UN and humanitarian agencies have called what is happening in Gaza a genocide, an intentional act to destroy, in whole or in part, a national, ethnic, racial, or religious group. Israel's leadership, including Prime Minister Netanyahu, has been accused of war crimes. But still, the word terrorism is absent.

It raises a chilling paradox: when the crime is massive enough, when it is executed by a state with power and allies, it becomes too large for the terrorism label to contain. The victims may be starved, bombed, displaced, but they are not recognised as victims of terror. Because the word, in practice, only moves one way, down the power hierarchy, never up.

And Gaza? Gaza becomes a ghost. A lesson in how suffering can be made invisible, legal, even rational, if the perpetrators hold the right passports.

## Section 6: - Starvation in Slow Motion: The Siege Economy Model

In modern warfare, the siege is no longer just about surrounding a city with troops. It is about surrounding a people with bureaucracy, policy, and sanctioned indifference. Starvation is no longer about empty shelves, it is about broken supply chains, blocked access permits, decimated infrastructure, and global complicity.

The siege economy is a 21st-century model of warfare, slow, grinding, and devastatingly effective. It does not need bullets or bombs. It needs red tape, fear, and delay.

From Gaza to Yemen, from Syria to Sudan, we are witnessing a chilling refinement of this model. The mechanisms are familiar: humanitarian aid is held hostage to political aims; food and medical supplies become bargaining chips; and entire populations are reduced to statistics, calories per day, litres of clean water per capita, infant mortality rates, school attendance. Behind each figure lies a deliberate strategy: deny, delay, disempower. The siege is no longer a military tactic, it is economic policy backed by diplomatic cover. And it is increasingly being deployed by states that wish to avoid the headlines of war while still waging one.

In Yemen, a Saudi-led blockade contributed to what the UN called the world's worst humanitarian crisis, with 80 per cent of the population needing aid. Fuel shortages crippled hospitals. Imports of food and medicine were restricted. Children died not from bullets but from wasting and diarrhoea. But Saudi Arabia remained a partner to the West, buying arms, hosting summits, shaking hands. It was hard to call them terrorists when they were also customers.

The siege economy is neat. It leaves no fingerprints. Governments can argue they are merely defending their borders, enforcing trade policy, applying security protocols. The suffering becomes ambient: long queues for bread, blackouts at hospitals, clean water only twice a week. No single moment shocks the conscience. But together, the effect is total: the erasure of the ability to live with dignity.

Meanwhile, media coverage wanes. Aid agencies lose funding. Foreign ministers express concern but avoid the word "famine," because famine implies failure, implies consequence, implies blame.

In Palestine, Israel's command of this siege economy is precise. The blockade of Gaza is enforced not only at the borders but through a web of permissions, blacklists, and arbitrary restrictions. Cement is banned in some periods, schoolbooks in others. International NGOs must negotiate daily access. Farmers are shot near buffer zones. Fishermen are fired on for crossing invisible lines. And yet, the justification remains consistent: "security." As though security is the opposite of humanity.

And still, no terrorism label is applied.

Contrast this with a rebel group stealing food convoys in a conflict zone. That is terror. That is looting aid. That is a war crime. But when a state restricts that aid entirely, using spreadsheets and border agents instead of machetes, it becomes policy. Regrettable, perhaps, but not terror.

This is the asymmetry. The rules are bent around the actor, not the act. A blockade by Hamas would be terrorism. A blockade by a sovereign state is geopolitics. A child starving in Aleppo draws sympathy. A child starving in Gaza draws suspicion. Was the parent a militant? Was the area a threat? The logic becomes circular: suffering is assumed to be self-inflicted if the oppressor wears a uniform.

The siege economy also gives plausible deniability. The suffering is indirect. Leaders claim to regret the civilian toll but insist the fault lies with the enemy. "They hide among civilians." "They refuse to surrender." "They are using food as a weapon." The projection is complete.

And while diplomats argue and NGOs scramble, the hunger deepens.

But there is one more element that ensures the siege economy continues unchecked: the apathy of those not under siege. The international community has mastered the art of concern without consequence. Statements of worry are not matched by sanctions or embargoes. The UN can declare a famine, but if no state moves to intervene, the famine becomes a footnote.

Starvation has become strategic, not as an accident of war, but as its method.

The question is no longer whether states can get away with it, but how many already are.

## Section 7: - Sanctions and the Illusion of Legitimacy

Sanctions occupy a unique space in the arsenal of statecraft. Unlike bombs or bullets, they arrive in the language of law, often cloaked in bureaucratic legitimacy and international procedures. They are portrayed not as acts of aggression, but as *tools of diplomacy*, non-violent measures designed to coerce states into changing behaviour without the need for open warfare. But scratch beneath that veneer, and a different picture emerges: one of systemic economic punishment, suffering inflicted on civilian populations, and a global double standard that shields the powerful while targeting the weak.

The illusion of legitimacy is central to how sanctions are sold to the public. Western governments and their allies argue that sanctions are a *peaceful* response to rogue regimes. They are framed as a middle path between inaction and war. Media outlets echo this framing, presenting sanctions as an unfortunate but necessary measure to uphold international law. Politicians refer to them as evidence of the *rules-based order* at work. But the consequences of these actions rarely make the headlines: hyperinflation, medicine shortages, food insecurity, the collapse of basic services, and the slow strangulation of entire economies.

Iraq in the 1990s stands as a haunting example. The UN sanctions regime, enforced primarily by the United States and the United Kingdom, lasted more than a decade and devastated the country's civilian infrastructure. A UNICEF report in 1999 estimated that more than 500,000 children had died due to the effects of sanctions: malnutrition, lack of access to clean water, and preventable disease. When then U.S. Secretary of State Madeleine Albright was asked whether the deaths were *worth it*, she replied, "We think the price is worth it." It was a moment that crystallised the moral incoherence of the sanctions narrative: the admission that mass civilian death could be justified in the name of strategic pressure.

Despite these humanitarian catastrophes, sanctions remain the preferred option for global powers seeking to punish adversaries without engaging in direct combat. Iran, Venezuela, North Korea, Syria—each has been subjected to wide-ranging sanctions that have done far more to punish ordinary citizens than to alter the behaviour of ruling elites. In many cases, authoritarian leaders use the sanctions as a propaganda tool, blaming foreign powers for domestic failings while the populace suffers in silence.

Meanwhile, allies of the West are rarely subjected to similar constraints. Israel's decades-long occupation of Palestinian territories, its expanding settlements deemed illegal under international law, and its military operations in Gaza have triggered no serious economic sanctions from the same actors who enforce crippling restrictions elsewhere. The double standard is glaring. It suggests that sanctions are not a neutral tool applied based on principle, but a selective weapon, targeting the weak, sparing the strong, and reflecting geopolitical alignments rather than moral imperatives.

The term *targeted sanctions* is another rhetorical device designed to deflect criticism. These are supposed to be carefully calibrated measures aimed at individuals or entities responsible for wrongdoing: freezing assets, banning travel, or limiting access to international finance. But in practice, the lines blur. Sanctions that aim to target a regime's leadership often disrupt entire economies.

Financial systems seize up. Foreign investment dries up. Food and medicine become scarce, not because of intentional malice, but because the system as a whole is paralysed. Humanitarian exemptions, where they exist, are often difficult to navigate, poorly implemented, and woefully inadequate.

Worse still, sanctions often have no clear endgame. Once imposed, they become politically difficult to lift. Leaders fear being seen as *soft* or as betraying victims. Bureaucracies ossify around sanctions regimes, and lobbyists emerge to defend their continuation. The original objectives are forgotten or evolve into moving targets. Over time, sanctions become an end in themselves, a symbol of moral posturing rather than a path to resolution.

And so the illusion persists. Sanctions are not bombs, we are told. They are the civilised response. But for the mother unable to obtain insulin for her child in Iran, or the father in Venezuela watching his wages dissolve into worthlessness, the distinction is academic. Sanctions kill just as surely as missiles do, only more slowly, and with the added cruelty of pretending it is not violence at all.

If a non-state actor were to impose economic deprivation on a civilian population—blocking their access to medicine, disrupting food supply chains, and collapsing their economy—what would we call it? Would we label it terrorism, a crime against humanity, an act of war? And if so, why do we not use the same language when states do it under the cover of international institutions?

This is the enduring hypocrisy of modern geopolitics: actions are judged not by their outcomes, but by the narrative that surrounds them. Sanctions have become the velvet glove over an iron fist, a form of structural violence with plausible deniability. And in that plausible deniability lies their greatest power and their greatest danger.

## Section 8 – The Disappearing Line Between Law and Punishment

One of the most disturbing consequences of siege tactics and economic sanctions is the erosion of the boundary between law and punishment. Traditionally, law is meant to serve justice, to uphold rights, and to constrain power. But in the era of global counter-terrorism and strategic embargoes, this function has been inverted. Legal instruments, particularly sanctions regimes, are now deployed as instruments of collective coercion rather than targeted accountability.

Consider the case of Iraq in the 1990s. Following the Gulf War, sweeping UN sanctions were imposed on the country with the stated aim of containing Saddam Hussein's regime and disarming Iraq of alleged weapons of mass destruction. But the human cost of these sanctions was catastrophic. UN officials estimated that over half a million children died as a result of restricted access to food, medicine, and basic supplies. When then-U.S. Secretary of State Madeleine Albright was asked in a 1996 *60 Minutes* interview whether the deaths of those children were *worth it*, she replied, "We think the price is worth it." It was a chilling moment of moral clarity, the admission that civilian suffering was not a regrettable consequence, but an accepted outcome of policy.

That episode revealed something deeper: when the line between civilian life and military objective is blurred, so too is the distinction between governance and vengeance. Sanctions become a blunt tool, applied not to influence behaviour with precision, but to punish en masse. The logic is not surgical but symbolic. It sends a message: defy us, and your people will suffer. Starvation becomes a strategy. Collapse becomes leverage.

This is not merely unethical; it undermines the legal frameworks that claim to uphold international order. The Geneva Conventions, for example, prohibit collective punishment. But how else can we describe sanctions that knowingly deprive entire populations of basic survival needs? Even when couched in bureaucratic language—*dual-use goods, sectoral targeting, compliance frameworks*—the effect remains the same. A population is forced to bear the consequences of political decisions it did not make and cannot reverse.

The same can be said of sieges in modern warfare, where access to food, fuel, and medicine is deliberately restricted. Israel's blockade of Gaza, for instance, has been described by some human rights organisations as *collective punishment on an unprecedented scale*. Israel claims it is a defensive measure, aimed at weakening Hamas. But the lived reality for over two million people, half of them children, is one of deprivation, fear, and entrapment. When power stations run dry and hospitals are forced to shut down, it ceases to matter whether the policy was technically lawful. What matters is the suffering it produces.

International law, if it is to retain legitimacy, must do more than codify violence with rules. It must guard against policies that are morally and practically indistinguishable from siege warfare. Otherwise, it becomes complicit in the very abuses it was meant to prevent.

What we see, again and again, is that the legal justification for starvation and sanctions often follows the political decision, not the other way around. Leaders act, then retroactively seek legal cover. The narrative of legitimacy is constructed after the fact, through language that sanitises violence and erases human cost. And the public, dulled by euphemisms and repetition, becomes complicit too.

The final tragedy is this: when law becomes a weapon of punishment rather than a shield of protection, it ceases to be law at all. It becomes policy in uniform, stripped of justice, hollowed of meaning, and wielded in service of power.

# CHAPTER SEVEN
# The Gaza Paradox

## Section 1: - A City Under Siege

Gaza is a place unlike any other. Just 25 miles long and 7 miles wide, it is home to over two million people, most of them refugees or descendants of refugees. It is often described as the world's largest open-air prison, sealed off by land, sea, and air. Goods and people do not move freely in or out. Electricity and clean water are rationed. Reconstruction materials are tightly controlled. Every few years, a new war brings fresh destruction to a place that never truly recovers.

Yet for all this, Gaza is rarely described in the language of occupation or humanitarian crisis. Instead, it is spoken of, particularly in the West, in the language of security and self-defence. When Israeli airstrikes kill hundreds of civilians, including children, we are told these are *targeted strikes* against militants. When a residential tower collapses in flames, it is a *regrettable consequence* of Hamas's presence. And when Gazans respond with crude rockets, it is called terrorism, full stop.

This is the Gaza paradox: a place that suffers acts indistinguishable from terrorism, but where the term is never applied to the state delivering the violence. The people being bombed are often called terrorists. The people dropping the bombs never are.

## Section 2: - The Language of Justification

After the October 2023 Hamas attack on Israel, the international narrative fell into familiar patterns. The attack was immediately, and rightly, condemned for its brutality. But the subsequent Israeli response, which killed thousands of Palestinians in Gaza and displaced hundreds of thousands more, was couched in the language of moral clarity. Israel was *defending itself*. Hamas had brought this upon the people. Civilian casualties, we were told, were tragic, but necessary in the fight against terror.

But what kind of fight is this?

Entire apartment blocks were flattened. Hospitals and UN-run schools were struck. Journalists, medics, and aid workers were killed in their homes and offices. These were not accidents. In many cases, warnings were not issued. In others, the targets had been shared in advance with Israeli forces to avoid such attacks. And yet they were hit anyway.

Still, the word *terrorism* was never applied. Not to the bombers. Not to the state. Not to the occupying power.

## Section 3: - Whose Lives Matter?

The death toll tells one story. The framing tells another.

A Palestinian rocket that kills three civilians is global news. An Israeli missile that kills thirty is a footnote. One is described as terror. The other as defence. This disparity is not accidental. It reflects a broader narrative hierarchy, in which some lives are implicitly more grievable than others, and some acts of violence more narratively valuable than others.

Edward Said once wrote that the Palestinians were *the victims of the victims*. This layered victimhood has created a moral fog in which even the most brutal Israeli actions are shielded by historical grievance and geopolitical alliances.

The world looks at Gaza and sees chaos. But chaos is not the absence of policy. It is often the result of it.

## Section 4: - The Terrorism Label Never Sticks

The fundamental question is this: if terrorism is defined as the intentional use of violence against civilians to achieve political aims, then why does it apply to Hamas but never to Israel?

Certainly, Hamas has committed acts that meet this definition. Suicide bombings. Rocket attacks. Civilian deaths. But when Israel responds with military force that produces far higher civilian casualties—often with overwhelming firepower, often targeting critical infrastructure—it is not considered terrorism. It is considered warfare. Legitimate. Strategic. Defensive.

This selective application of the term betrays its true function. It is not about the act. It is about the actor. The term *terrorism* sticks to the stateless, the poor, the politically inconvenient. It slides off the powerful, the aligned, the Western-approved.

This is why, in the aftermath of horrific bombings in Gaza, the question is never whether Israel is committing terrorism. The only question is whether it is "proportionate".

## Section 5: - The Question Netanyahu Refused to Answer

At a press conference in late 2023, Benjamin Netanyahu was asked by an international journalist whether Palestinians had the right to defend themselves. His answer was stark: "No."

The room fell silent. There was no attempt to couch the answer in legal nuance or humanitarian concern. The right to resist occupation, it seemed, applied only to the occupier. The oppressed had no such claim.

This moment crystallised the paradox. A stateless people under siege, subjected to repeated military assaults, were denied even the theoretical right to self-defence. Their every action, no matter how desperate, was framed as terror. Meanwhile, the state inflicting the violence enjoyed the benefit of legal structures, media sympathy, and geopolitical cover.

The term *terrorism* had become so malleable, so politicised, that its application was no longer tied to behaviour but to allegiance.

## Section 6: - Moral Clarity or Moral Collapse?

The greatest danger of the Gaza paradox is not just the immediate suffering. It is the long-term corrosion of moral standards. When entire families can be wiped out and the world shrugs, when mass displacement is justified as a strategic necessity, when starvation and siege are reframed as tools of counter-terrorism, we lose more than lives. We lose the credibility of our humanitarian ideals.

Gaza is not a distant battlefield. It is a mirror. It reflects our values back to us, and the image is not flattering. It asks whether the global order truly cares about international law or whether such law is only enforced when it serves powerful interests.

If violence against civilians is wrong, it must be wrong regardless of the flag under which it is committed. If killing innocents to achieve political aims is terrorism, then it cannot matter whether the perpetrator wears a uniform or carries a mandate.

But that is not how the world operates. In Gaza, we see the exception becoming the rule. In the silence of international institutions, in the evasions of the media, in the passivity of those who claim moral leadership, we see not moral clarity but moral collapse.

# CHAPTER EIGHT

## Section 1: – The Violence We Forgot

History is not a record of what happened. It is a story we choose to tell about what happened, and, just as importantly, what we choose to forget. Every nation has its own version of "the good fight," the noble war, the just cause. But lurking behind the myths are the silences: massacres rebranded as battles, atrocities written off as accidents, entire peoples who simply vanish from the national story.

It is easy to see how this selective amnesia serves those in power. When violence is committed by the state, particularly in the name of national security or civilising missions, the instinct is not to name it for what it was but to bury it beneath a narrative of heroism or necessity. The result is a long global history of state-led brutality that never meets the threshold of "terrorism," not because the acts are different, but because the perpetrators wrote the script.

Think about how we teach history in schools. The French Revolution is valorised, the Haitian Revolution less so. The World Wars are remembered with solemn pride, but the colonial campaigns that supported them in Africa, Asia, and the Middle East are often omitted or glossed over. In the UK, schoolchildren learn about the Blitz, but few learn about the firebombing of Dresden. Americans honour D-Day but skip over the napalm dropped on Vietnamese villages. It is not that the facts are unavailable. It is that they are not included in the story we choose to tell ourselves.

Why? Because national identity is, in part, built on clean hands. To admit to terrorism, or even atrocity, on the part of the state is to fracture the moral legitimacy upon which authority depends. It is far more palatable to claim that these events were unfortunate outcomes of war, isolated errors, or justified responses to provocation. The dead become collateral. The killers become misunderstood heroes.

But there is a cost to forgetting. When state violence is not only excused but celebrated, it sets a precedent: that so long as you win, the morality of your methods does not matter. That only the violence of the other is to be feared, condemned, and named. And that is how historical amnesia becomes not just a failure of memory but a weapon of power.

## Section 2 – Wounded Knee: A Massacre with Medals

On the frozen plains of South Dakota in December 1890, the U.S. 7th Cavalry surrounded a Lakota Sioux encampment near Wounded Knee Creek. They had come to disarm the tribe, whose people, cold, hungry, and afraid, had already been pushed to the brink of survival by decades of broken treaties, land seizures, and military campaigns. By the end of the day, at least 250 Native Americans lay dead, many of them women and children. Some were shot at close range. Others were pursued and gunned down as they fled.

It was a massacre. And yet, the United States government would not call it that. Instead, it awarded twenty Medals of Honor, the nation's highest military decoration, to the soldiers involved. To this day, those medals have not been revoked.

Why does this matter in a book about terrorism?

Because it reveals something essential about how we define violence. Had this same act, the mass killing of civilians, the pursuit and slaughter of the wounded, the firing upon unarmed families, been carried out by an insurgent group, it would be the textbook definition of terrorism. It would be listed on global databases, studied by security analysts, and invoked as a justification for sweeping counter-terror measures. But when it was committed by the state, in uniform, under a flag, it became history, not terrorism. Honourable, not criminal.

In 2025, U.S. Secretary of Defense Pete Hegseth was asked whether those medals should be rescinded. He said no. A review panel had agreed they were earned. The implication was clear: the act may have been regrettable, but it was legitimate. Necessary, even. There was no need to question the moral framework or the label.

But imagine for a moment the roles reversed. Imagine a Native American resistance group had attacked a U.S. military outpost and killed 250 people, including civilians, women, and children. Would they not be declared terrorists? Hunted across borders? Tried or executed without ceremony?

This is not about relitigating history. It is about recognising the rules we apply or suspend based on who holds power. The events at Wounded Knee expose the dangerous elasticity of the word terrorism. When states kill, they award medals. When the powerless resist, they are branded forever.

And the narrative moves on.

## Section 3 – My Lai: Terror by Another Name

It was March 16, 1968, in the tiny Vietnamese hamlet of My Lai. American soldiers from Charlie Company entered the village, expecting to encounter Viet Cong fighters. Instead, they found unarmed civilians, mostly women, children, and the elderly. By the time the sun set, over 500 villagers had been killed. Some were shot in ditches. Others were raped before execution. Babies were tossed in the air and impaled on bayonets. The massacre lasted four hours. No enemy fire was ever recorded.

And yet, this was not called terrorism.

The official narrative, at first, tried to hide what had happened. The U.S. Army reported a "fierce firefight" and "128 Viet Cong killed." Only when whistleblowers like Ron Ridenhour and soldiers like Hugh Thompson, a helicopter pilot who intervened to stop the killings, came forward did the truth emerge. Even then, accountability was rare. Of the dozens of soldiers involved, only one, Lieutenant William Calley, was convicted. He served just three and a half years under house arrest.

How can such horror escape the terrorism label?

Because once again, the act was judged by the actor: a state, a uniform, a flag. The same criteria reframe horror as "collateral damage," or in this case, a tragic exception. Not systemic, not ideological, not terroristic.

And yet, what is terrorism if not the use of violence and fear against civilians to achieve a political or military aim? The Vietnam War was precisely that, a campaign of overwhelming force designed to suppress a population deemed sympathetic to communism. The bombing of villages, the use of napalm and Agent Orange, the routine torching of homes—all served the purpose of breaking morale and eliminating resistance.

But this was not called terrorism. It was called policy.

Let us imagine again. If a non-state group had entered a village, slaughtered over 500 civilians, raped women, executed children, and boasted of it as a blow to their enemies, how would it be described? Would anyone hesitate to call it terror?

The My Lai massacre forces us to confront the double standard. It reminds us that violence does not cease to be terrorism because it is wrapped in a flag. It does not become less terrifying because it came from a trained army rather than a ragtag militia. In fact, the ability of a state to cover up such horror only magnifies its power to shape the narrative and to exempt itself from the moral consequences of its actions.

This is what makes state terror so potent. Not only does it inflict death, it controls the story of that death.

## Section 4 – Remembering Some, Forgetting Others

History is not just written by the victors; it is curated by them. What we remember, and what we conveniently forget, is a form of narrative warfare. In museums, history books, school curricula, and national commemorations, certain stories are elevated as honourable and necessary. Others vanish, buried beneath the weight of selective memory.

Consider the names that are etched in bronze: Normandy, Iwo Jima, Kabul. We are taught to remember the sacrifice, the courage, the necessity of these operations. But where are the memorials to the victims of Fallujah, or Kandahar, or the refugee camps bombed by drones in Yemen? Why do we remember the lives lost in 9/11 with solemn reverence, yet barely register the tens of thousands of innocent civilians killed in the retaliatory wars that followed?

This is not by accident. It is how states maintain moral authority. By enshrining some deaths as tragedies and others as statistical footnotes, they preserve the illusion of righteousness. State violence, even when grotesque, is explained, justified, and ultimately absorbed into the national story. Non-state violence, even when symbolic or reactive, is framed as aberrant, evil, and terroristic.

And here is the crux: terrorism is not just defined by who pulls the trigger; it is defined by who writes the history. Take, for instance, the bombing of Pan Am Flight 103 over Lockerbie. One of the most infamous acts of terrorism in modern history, carried out, we are told, by Libyan agents. The dead were mourned, their names remembered, and justice pursued across decades. Contrast this with the USS Vincennes' downing of Iran Air Flight 655 in 1988, which killed 290 innocent civilians. The U.S. never formally apologised. The captain of the ship received a medal. The victims were forgotten by all but their families and a few footnotes in academic journals.

Why does one event remain a cornerstone of the public understanding of terrorism, while the other fades into oblivion?

Because memory is not neutral. It is constructed.

This weaponisation of memory allows states to continue violent practices without enduring the reputational cost. It conditions future generations to view their nation's actions through a prism of benevolence while demonising the resistance of others as irrational hatred or extremism. The next time a drone strike wipes out a wedding party, the public shrugs; it does not even register. But if a homemade bomb goes off in a Western capital, the world demands blood.

Such is the power of forgetting. It cleans the hands of the powerful and ensures the repetition of the same horrors without consequence.

## Section 5 – Terror and Triumph: The Medals of Empire

The clearest sign of a world turned upside down is when the perpetrators of mass violence are not only absolved but celebrated.

We are told that terrorism is the domain of fanatics, criminals, cowards. And yet, throughout history, the bloodiest acts of violence have been committed not by insurgents in the shadows but by states in broad daylight. Even more grotesquely, such acts are often rewarded, not condemned.

Take the 1890 Wounded Knee Massacre. Hundreds of Lakota Sioux men, women, and children were slaughtered by U.S. cavalry forces. Their only crime was assembling unarmed at the tail end of a centuries-long campaign of extermination. Rather than face investigation, the soldiers responsible were awarded Medals of Honor, America's highest military distinction. This was not a rogue act. It was an affirmation of state policy. And in 2025, U.S. Secretary of Defense Pete Hegseth reaffirmed that decision. "They earned them," he said. The review panel had agreed. No apology. No retraction. Just more medals for a massacre.

The message is clear: violence committed in uniform, under the banner of the state, is not terrorism; it is honourable, even when it involves the systematic slaughter of civilians.

Now imagine the reverse. What if a Native resistance group had encircled a U.S. military outpost and killed hundreds of sleeping troops and their families? Would they have received medals? Or would they have been labelled the most monstrous terrorists in history?

The same double standard persists today. In Gaza, thousands of civilians have been killed in airstrikes—mothers, babies, doctors, journalists—all caught in the fog of "precision bombing." Israel claims self-defence. Western allies nod approvingly. And when Benjamin Netanyahu is accused of war crimes or even genocide, the terrorism label never sticks. It does not even appear. Yet a teenager with a rock, or a social media post supporting Hamas, is fair game for arrest, surveillance, or even execution by drone.

It is hard to think of a clearer expression of this absurdity than when awards and honours are bestowed for the taking of innocent life, provided it is done by those deemed "civilised."

The British Empire, too, left behind a trail of medals gleaming with blood. From the Amritsar Massacre to the suppression of the Mau Mau uprising in Kenya, imperial violence was not only sanctioned but decorated. The Victoria Cross, the Iron Cross, the Legion of Merit—all symbols of bravery draped over acts of terror when committed by the right people under the right flag.

State violence is not merely excused; it is mythologised. Taught in schools. Etched in granite. Remembered as triumph.

And so the state writes the story not just with bombs and bullets but with parades, statues, and citations. In doing so, it ensures that the most terroristic acts of all are never called by that name. They are victories. They are necessary. They are glorious.

They are never terrorism.

## Section 6 – The Unwritten Victims

History is often written by the victors, but even more crucially, it is omitted by the powerful. In the great ledgers of war, conquest, and state-building, there are blank pages where the victims should be.

When the British troops fired on unarmed Indians in Amritsar in 1919, killing at least 379 and injuring over a thousand, the official response was muted. General Dyer, who ordered the massacre, was not punished; in fact, he was celebrated by sections of the British public. Fundraisers were held in his honour. Newspapers praised his "firmness." The people of Amritsar were told their suffering had preserved the Raj.

But the victims were never named. Their stories were rarely told. Their families received no justice, only silence.

This pattern is tragically familiar.

In Vietnam, the My Lai Massacre saw over 500 civilians— mostly women, children, and the elderly—brutally killed by U.S. soldiers. Some were mutilated. Others raped. A few survivors crawled beneath the bodies of relatives to escape. The event was hidden for over a year until a whistleblower forced the story into the public eye. Even then, only one man—Lieutenant William Calley— was convicted. He served just three and a half years under house arrest.

The dead were left uncounted, unnamed, forgotten.

Fast forward to Gaza, Fallujah, or Yemen. Airstrikes level hospitals. Drones fire missiles into homes. Children die in their beds. And yet, the official reports speak of "neutralising targets" and "surgical operations." The victims vanish into euphemism.

No names. No photos. No mourning.

This is the narrative strategy of power: dehumanise the dead, erase their dignity, and you erase the question of guilt. You erase the possibility that the act could ever be called terrorism.

After all, can there be terror if no one admits that people were terrorised?

This is not just about the past. It is about how entire communities and nations are conditioned to accept that some deaths matter less. That some lives are footnotes. That a man killed by a drone in Waziristan was probably a terrorist. That a starving child in Gaza is a regrettable statistic. That a dead journalist in Ukraine or a wounded doctor in Sudan are unfortunate, but not reason enough to challenge the moral clarity of the state.

This silence is not accidental. It is designed. A strategic void where scrutiny might otherwise dwell.

We are told terrorism must be confronted. But when states commit acts of brutal violence, their victims are not granted even the recognition of being harmed. They become the unwritten.

And without their story, the lie endures.

## Section 7 – When Justice Looks the Other Way

The law is supposed to be blind. But in the theatre of terrorism and state violence, it often seems to wear selective lenses, sharp and punitive for the stateless, blurred and forgiving for the state.

Consider the principle of universal jurisdiction, which allows countries to prosecute individuals for grave crimes like genocide, torture, and crimes against humanity, regardless of where they occurred. In theory, it is a tool for justice without borders. In practice, it is rarely used against those backed by power.

The United States has consistently exempted itself from the jurisdiction of the International Criminal Court (ICC). In fact, under the American Service-Members' Protection Act—dubbed the "Hague Invasion Act"—the U.S. reserves the right to use military force to free any of its personnel held by the ICC. Justice, it seems, has territorial limits.

And then there is Israel, where war crimes allegations have been repeatedly raised over operations in Gaza. Civilian infrastructure destroyed. Entire families wiped out in a single airstrike. Hospitals bombed. U.N. schools flattened. These acts, documented by reputable international bodies, have drawn condemnation. But terrorism? Never uttered.

Prime Minister Benjamin Netanyahu has been accused of war crimes. But terrorism? No. That word is reserved for Palestinians with home-made rockets, not states with fighter jets. The narrative is policed not just by governments, but by courts, tribunals, and legal doctrine. Terrorism, we are told, cannot be committed by a state.

That, too, is a fiction.

When courts in the Global South have attempted to investigate Western or allied states for possible war crimes, they have faced immense pressure. Funding withdrawn. Judges intimidated. Witnesses disappeared. The machinery of international justice, under such strain, often stalls. Or worse, acquiesces.

Meanwhile, local laws in democratic states have become tools to criminalise dissent. Peaceful protesters charged under anti-terror legislation. Whistleblowers prosecuted for revealing state abuses. Journalists surveilled and silenced in the name of "national security."

In the UK, Palestine Action activists—some of them clergy, some elderly—have been arrested and prosecuted for non-violent direct action against arms companies. Their acts of protest are labelled "terror-related offences." Their trials are framed not as civil disobedience but as threats to the state.

The irony is stark: when the powerless resist, they are terror suspects. When the powerful kill, they are beyond reproach.

Justice, in this domain, is not just blind; it has been instructed to look the other way.

## Section 8 – The Memory Hole

History, George Orwell warned, is not just written by the victors, it is rewritten by them. In his dystopian world of *1984*, uncomfortable truths were fed into the "memory hole," incinerated to make way for more convenient lies. That was fiction. But in the world of real-world terrorism narratives, the memory hole is very much alive. Events that challenge the dominant narrative of "us = civilisation, them = terror" are quietly discarded, minimised, or retroactively rebranded. Not because they did not happen, but because remembering them accurately is too politically inconvenient.

Take the My Lai massacre in Vietnam. Over 500 unarmed civilians—men, women, children, even infants—were gunned down by U.S. troops in 1968. Bodies mutilated. Women raped. Babies bayoneted. One soldier, Lieutenant William Calley, was convicted. He served just three years under house arrest. The rest were quietly returned to service or never charged at all. To this day, My Lai is taught, if at all, as an aberration, a "mistake," rather than terrorism. Collateral. Unfortunate. Never deliberate.

Or consider Fallujah in Iraq, 2004. The U.S. military used white phosphorus munitions in a heavily populated city, chemical weapons banned under international law. Civilians suffered horrendous burns. Entire neighbourhoods were flattened. Yet no senior figure was held accountable. The term terrorism was not just avoided, it was unimaginable.

Meanwhile, entire historical episodes that could expose the hypocrisy of terrorism labels are airbrushed. The British Empire's scorched-earth tactics in Kenya. The French torture campaigns during the Algerian War. The CIA's sponsorship of death squads in Latin America. All violent. All ideological. All designed to spread fear and crush opposition. But terrorism? Never officially recorded as such.

Memory is selective because power is selective. What we remember shapes what we believe, and what we believe determines whom we fear and whom we forgive.

This is why museums of state violence are rare. Why archives are redacted. Why some victims are remembered with solemnity and others not at all. It is why the Wounded Knee Massacre still carries U.S. Medals of Honor. And why the victims of Gaza will likely never see justice, let alone memorialisation.

We speak of a global war on terror, but we rarely ask: whose terror? Whose war? Whose stories are allowed to survive the telling?

In the end, the biggest casualty may not be the victims; it may be the truth itself, quietly disappearing down a hole in our collective memory.

# CONCLUSION TO PART II: -
# When the State Is Violent

If Part I of this book exposed the ambiguity and manipulation of the word "terrorism," Part II has shown how that ambiguity becomes lethal when monopolised by the state. We have seen how powerful nations justify brutality, excusing mass death as collateral, framing starvation as strategy, and erasing atrocity through selective memory. The victims of these actions, often voiceless, stateless, or simply on the wrong side of a political alliance, are not just killed; they are disqualified from even being mourned.

Yet the states that commit such acts never bear the terrorist label. They operate behind walls of legal jargon, diplomatic immunity, and narrative control. The same violence that would earn a non-state actor eternal condemnation becomes, when state sanctioned, policy, defence, security, or peacekeeping.

But people do fight back. And that is where we turn next.

**Introduction to Part III: Protest, Resistance, and Rebellion**

When the state decides who is a terrorist, then those who resist the state, even non-violently, are often next in line for the label. Around the world, from Gaza to Minneapolis, from London to Kashmir, resistance movements are branded not by what they do but by whom they challenge. Protest becomes extremism. Solidarity becomes sedition. Rebellion, even when rooted in justice, becomes indistinguishable from terror, not in reality but in rhetoric.

And yet history tells us that many of yesterday's terrorists are today's statesmen. Many of the world's most celebrated liberation movements, from anti-colonial uprisings in Africa to civil rights struggles in the United States, were denounced as dangerous, disruptive, and even terrorist by those in power at the time.

113

So what happens when the people rise and the state calls it terrorism?

In Part III, we examine that fraught space between protest and prosecution, rebellion and repression, and ask:

*Can freedom fighting survive the age of counter-terrorism?*

# PART III

# CHAPTER NINE

## Section 1: Framing the Fighter

What makes someone a terrorist? Is it the weapon they use, the cause they fight for, or the uniform they wear, or do not wear?

History is full of figures who straddled the line between villain and hero, terrorist and freedom fighter, depending entirely on who was doing the telling. Think of Nelson Mandela, once branded a terrorist by the United States and the United Kingdom for his leadership of the armed wing of the African National Congress. He spent 27 years in prison. Then he emerged, was elected president, and became a global symbol of peace and reconciliation. Did his actions change, or was it only the story told about them?

This is the enduring tension at the heart of modern politics. Violence by the weak is often called terrorism, while violence by the powerful is called law enforcement, peacekeeping or self-defence. The Palestinian child throwing a rock at a tank is committing violence. The soldier in the tank, returning fire, is defending himself. Who is the aggressor? Who is the oppressed? Who gets to decide?

It is not simply a matter of tactics. Guerrilla warfare, sabotage and even bombings have been the tools of the desperate and the occupied for centuries. From the French Resistance during Nazi occupation to the Irish Republican Army during The Troubles, and to anti-colonial fighters across Africa and Asia, the story of national liberation has often been written in blood. Yet the way these stories are told depends not on what was done, but on what was achieved and on who writes the final chapter.

Western powers, in particular, have a long history of shifting the narrative. The United States lauds George Washington as a founding father, yet to the British Empire he was a rebel commander leading a violent insurrection. Men like Menachem Begin, who ordered the bombing of the King David Hotel in 1946, killing 91 people, later became Prime Minister of Israel. Once a terrorist, then a statesman.

And herein lies the difficulty. Terrorism is not a fixed moral category; it is a political one. The same person can move from outlaw to leader, from hunted to honoured, from imprisoned to inaugurated, with nothing more than a shift in power and a rewrite of the story.

Even in contemporary conflicts, we see this tension unfold. Ukrainian resistance fighters are praised in Western media for using Molotov cocktails and improvised explosives against Russian troops. Yet similar tactics used by Palestinian militants are condemned outright as terrorism. The acts are nearly identical. The narrative is not.

This selective framing has deep consequences. It shapes who receives support, who receives funding, who is targeted by drone strikes, and who is granted asylum. It influences how children are taught history, how laws are written and how foreign policy is decided. It determines whether the world watches with sympathy or looks away in fear.

The phrase *One man's terrorist is another man's freedom fighter* may sound tired, but it holds a mirror to the hypocrisy we are asked to accept. It reminds us that moral clarity is not always possible, and that, more often than not, it is not even attempted. Instead, what we receive is narrative dominance. And the winners write the story.

So what happens when the powerful lose control of that story? When the oppressed begin to speak, to film, to tweet? When the images of bombed hospitals and starving children challenge the official version of events?

This is the battle of the twenty-first century: not only over territory, but over truth. Not only over violence, but over vocabulary. And it begins with asking uncomfortable questions about who we call a terrorist, and why.

## Section 2: - The Role of Empire in Shaping the Label

Empires have always controlled more than land and people; they have controlled language. In the age of conquest, it was not enough to defeat your enemy militarily, you had to define them morally. The labels *savage*, *barbarian* and later *terrorist* became critical tools of imperial power. By labelling resistance as illegitimate, or criminal, empires justified their own violence as righteous, civilising and necessary.

This dynamic is especially visible in the British Empire's long history of suppressing uprisings. From India to Kenya, from Ireland to Palestine, Britain was repeatedly confronted with local populations fighting for independence. Rarely were these rebels understood through the lens of political grievance or national aspiration. Instead, they were often branded thugs, criminals or extremists, or the preferred term after the twentieth century, terrorists.

Consider the Mau Mau uprising in Kenya during the 1950s. What began as a demand for land reform and national liberation was painted by the British government and press as a campaign of mindless violence. Colonial authorities detained tens of thousands of Kenyans in camps, many of whom were tortured or killed, yet the British narrative was one of restoring order against savagery. The atrocities committed by the empire were sanitised; the resistance of the oppressed was demonised. It took until 2013 for the UK government to formally acknowledge and apologise for the abuse.

The same can be said of the Irish struggle. During the 1916 Easter Rising, Irish republicans who sought independence from

British rule were described as traitors and terrorists, even as they declared a republic and issued a political proclamation. The subsequent execution of its leaders helped galvanise Irish public opinion, but Britain's language remained unchanged. Those who challenged imperial rule were dangerous and illegitimate. That narrative continued through The Troubles, as successive UK governments refused to recognise the political motivations of the IRA, even while negotiating with them privately.

Post-imperial powers like France and the United States have followed similar patterns. The French labelled Algerian independence fighters as terrorists throughout the 1954 to 1962 war, even while employing brutal torture and mass repression to hold on to the colony. In Vietnam, American forces described Viet Cong insurgents as terrorists, while U.S. operations such as Operation Rolling Thunder and the My Lai Massacre caused mass civilian casualties.

The pattern is clear. Those who resist empire are almost always labelled terrorists. And that label remains long after the war is over. It becomes embedded in history books, media coverage and political discourse. It shapes who is remembered as a freedom fighter and who is forgotten or vilified.

This framing is not accidental. It is a deliberate strategy of narrative control. If you can persuade the world that your enemy is not merely opposed to you, but to civilisation itself, then your own violence becomes morally necessary. You are no longer an occupier; you are a defender of order. You are not suppressing independence; you are combating terror.

This manipulation extends into modern counter-terrorism frameworks. The post-9/11 world saw the rapid expansion of anti-terror laws that echoed colonial-era logic: profiling, pre-emptive detention, the criminalisation of protest and the globalisation of surveillance. And, much like empire, the West continues to reserve for itself the right to define who is a terrorist and who is a partner in peace.

Meanwhile, the victims of that imperial framing, those once labelled terrorists, have sometimes managed to reclaim their narrative. Mandela. Gandhi. Kenyatta. Collins. But many others remain buried beneath the weight of the label, their names unspoken, their cause forever tainted by the language of terror.

The empire may be gone in name, but its vocabulary survives. And it still shapes the global conversation.

## Section 3: - The Empire's Shadow – Sachs on the Roots of Modern Terror

In a striking lecture delivered to the UN Security Council in 2023, Professor Jeffrey Sachs, renowned economist and global policy expert, offered a sobering assessment of the world's ongoing unrest. He did not point the finger at rogue militias, fanatical ideologues, or even religious extremism. Instead, he cast his gaze backward, firmly and unflinchingly, at the legacy of European imperialism, with Britain squarely in the frame. According to Sachs, many of the world's enduring conflicts, from the Middle East to South Asia and parts of Africa, can trace their origins to the political borders, sectarian divisions, and institutional fragility engineered by the British Empire.

It is a radical claim at first glance. But scratch beneath the surface of today's most violent and unstable regions, and imperial fingerprints are everywhere. In Palestine, the Balfour Declaration and British Mandate set in motion a century of displacement and resentment. In Iraq and Syria, borders drawn with colonial indifference ignored ethnic and religious identities, sowing the seeds of division. In India and Pakistan, Partition unleashed a bloodbath that reverberates through Kashmir to this day. In Northern Ireland,

British policy institutionalised sectarian inequality for generations, fuelling decades of violent resistance and state repression.

Sachs' argument is not simply that Britain made historical mistakes. It is that the very design of empire—divide and rule, extraction over development, dominance without consent—created structural conditions in which violence became a rational response. People who were denied agency, whose identities were suppressed or manipulated, and whose resources were plundered, often saw no recourse but resistance. And when they did resist, the label of "terrorist" was ready and waiting for them.

Consider the Mau Mau rebellion in Kenya during the 1950s. The British government framed it as a terrorist insurgency and responded with mass detentions, torture and executions. Yet decades later, the UK government paid compensation to survivors, tacitly acknowledging the brutality of its counterinsurgency. Were the Mau Mau terrorists, or anti-colonial freedom fighters? The same question applies to the Irish Republican Army, the African National Congress in apartheid-era South Africa, and countless other groups whose violent resistance emerged from colonial injustice.

What Sachs adds to this discourse is not just historical blame but an urgent call to honesty. His plea to world leaders was not to relitigate empire for the sake of guilt, but to recognise how imperial legacies continue to shape global governance, inequality and conflict. He warns that without this reckoning, Western powers will continue to misdiagnose the causes of unrest, seeing it as senseless terrorism rather than the predictable outgrowth of long-standing injustice.

The power of Sachs' framing lies in its inversion of the usual question. Instead of asking why people turn to violence, he asks why we are surprised when they do. Why are we shocked that peoples dispossessed, ignored and humiliated by empire still carry trauma, and that this trauma finds expression in resistance, sometimes violent? Why do we continue to treat terrorism as an isolated pathology rather than as a political consequence?

In many ways, Sachs' critique dovetails with earlier post-colonial thinkers, from Frantz Fanon to Edward Said, who viewed terrorism not as a disease, but as a symptom. Fanon, writing on Algeria, described violence as the colonised person's final assertion of selfhood in a world where all other avenues had been denied. Sachs updates that argument for a modern audience, placing it in a globalised context of policy failures, economic disparity and military overreach. In doing so, he reframes terrorism not as a cultural or religious aberration, but as the unfinished business of empire.

This perspective challenges the core of how we categorise and condemn violence. It suggests that the "war on terror" may in fact be a war against the consequences of Western history. It raises uncomfortable questions for former imperial powers. If the wounds of empire still fester, can you condemn the infection without acknowledging the injury?

To ignore Sachs' warning is to persist in a dangerous illusion. Violence does not simply erupt out of hatred or fanaticism. It does not arrive without context or cause. Context matters. History matters. And without them, the label of "terrorist" becomes a convenient cloak that hides our complicity.

In this murky world, where states kill without consequence and individuals are branded forever for resistance, Sachs forces us to reckon with a different narrative. One in which the lines between oppressor and terrorist are not just blurred, but drawn, erased and redrawn by the hands of history.

## Section 4: - Sympathisers and the Slippery Slope of Solidarity

In an age of binary thinking, us versus them, good versus evil, solidarity has become a dangerous act. No longer merely an expression of empathy, it can be recast as allegiance. A slogan, a tweet, a donation to the wrong cause, or even showing up at the wrong protest, can be enough to draw accusations of being a "sympathiser." The word implies not just support, but guilt by association, a subtle shift with profound consequences.

It is a tactic that has proven especially effective in the age of the "War on Terror." You do not have to be a terrorist to be treated like one. You only need to be perceived as sympathetic to a cause that challenges the prevailing narrative.

Take, for example, the aftermath of the October 7 Hamas attack in 2023. Israeli officials, led by Prime Minister Benjamin Netanyahu and National Security Minister Itamar Ben-Gvir, made sweeping declarations that "there are no innocents in Gaza." This chilling statement implied a moral free-for-all, that every man, woman, and child in the strip was either a terrorist or a terrorist sympathiser, and therefore a legitimate target. It was not just a justification for war, but a justification for erasing ethical restraint. In such a worldview, proportionality, civilian protection, and international law no longer apply. They are luxuries denied to sympathisers.

This logic has a long history. In Northern Ireland, during the Troubles, entire Catholic communities were branded as IRA sympathisers. Internment without trial, the use of the Special Powers Act, mass surveillance, and brutal counter-insurgency tactics were justified on the basis that the population harboured terrorists. As former Sinn Féin leader Gerry Adams once put it: "The British didn't just treat republicans as terrorists, they treated all of us as terrorists in waiting."

Across the Atlantic, in the United States, Donald Trump frequently invoked the language of guilt by association during his first and second terms. He labelled Black Lives Matter a "terrorist organisation" and referred to Antifa activists as "violent anarchists." Peaceful protestors were gassed and beaten under the pretext that they were domestic enemies. Even elderly religious figures were not spared. Ninety-one-year-old nuns arrested for Palestine Action protests in the UK were accused of supporting terrorism, simply for opposing arms sales to Israel.

This weaponisation of the label extends to institutions. UNRWA, the UN agency providing humanitarian aid in Gaza, was defunded by multiple Western governments after Israel claimed, without conclusive evidence, that some of its staff had links to Hamas. Netanyahu's accusation was enough. No trial. No investigation. Just defunding. Again, guilt by association.

In a climate where governments and media are primed to believe the worst of the powerless, the mere suggestion of connection becomes damning. Palestinian solidarity events on university campuses in the UK and US have been branded as "hate rallies." Students have been suspended. Donors have pulled funding. In one instance, a professor lost her job after sharing an article that criticised Israel's military operations. No bombs. No threats. Just a share button.

The doctrine of "no innocents" now operates in political discourse as much as in military strategy. It transforms people who advocate for justice into enablers of terror. It leaves no space for complexity, for understanding root causes, for peaceful protest. You are either with us or with the terrorists. That is the logic.

It is worth remembering that the apartheid regime in South Africa used the same rhetoric. Nelson Mandela was imprisoned for 27 years, not because of proven violence, but because of his association with the armed wing of the ANC. He was branded a terrorist and remained on the US terrorist watchlist until 2008, 14 years after becoming South Africa's president.

What these cases reveal is a chilling pattern. The line between citizen and criminal, protestor and terrorist, is not drawn by action, but by politics. Once that line is crossed in the eyes of the state, everything becomes permissible.

As Professor Judith Butler once observed: "Who counts as a human? Whose lives are grievable?" The sympathiser doctrine provides a clear answer: only those who do not challenge the status quo.

## Section 5: - The 'No Innocents' Doctrine – Erasing the Civilian

One of the most insidious evolutions in modern counterterrorism discourse is the quiet abandonment of the distinction between combatants and civilians. The moral firewall that once protected non-combatants, even in times of war, is being steadily dismantled by the rhetorical force of the "no innocents" doctrine.

This is not just careless language. It is an intentional reframing of entire populations as legitimate targets, using the claim of universal complicity. In doing so, states absolve themselves of responsibility for civilian deaths and redefine atrocity as strategy.

The most brazen example in recent memory comes from Israel's conduct in Gaza. In the weeks following the October 7 Hamas attack, Israeli officials repeatedly insisted there were "no innocent civilians" in Gaza. Itamar Ben-Gvir, the Israeli Minister for National Security, went so far as to declare, "There are no uninvolved civilians in Gaza." This was not a slip of the tongue. It was a calculated political message: the entire population is implicated. Everyone is a legitimate target.

Once such framing takes hold, it becomes remarkably easy to justify actions that would otherwise be condemned. A flattened apartment block is not a massacre, it is a strike on a neighbourhood of sympathisers. A destroyed hospital is not a war crime, it is collateral damage in a war against human shields. The logic is circular and self-reinforcing: if all Gazans are terrorists, then killing them cannot be terrorism.

This principle has deep roots. During the Vietnam War, the U.S. military operated under the unofficial but chilling motto: "Kill them all, let God sort them out." Villages were razed, and civilians were often presumed guilty by geography. The My Lai massacre, in which over 500 unarmed civilians were killed, was initially covered up by the Pentagon. Even when exposed, the primary perpetrator, Lt. William Calley, served only three and a half years under house arrest.

In Iraq, during the early 2000s, U.S. counterinsurgency forces treated Sunni populations in Anbar Province as suspect en masse. The presumption was that sympathy with insurgents equalled complicity. Raids, detentions, and airstrikes were executed on vague suspicions. Entire neighbourhoods became "hostile zones." Innocence was no longer presumed, it had to be proven.

The logic extended to U.S. drone policy under successive presidents, including Obama and Trump. Leaked documents revealed that any "military-aged male" in a strike zone was automatically considered an enemy combatant unless posthumous evidence proved otherwise. This is Orwellian justice: you are guilty until dead and only then, possibly, found innocent.

The 'no innocents' doctrine also appears in state responses to domestic protest. In Turkey, Erdoğan's government used the attempted coup of 2016 to round up tens of thousands of civil servants, teachers, journalists, and academics, claiming they were supporters of terrorism through association with the Gülen movement. Families were destroyed, careers ended, dissent silenced. Again, innocence was irrelevant. The state had drawn a line and everything on the other side was terrorism.

This dangerous mindset is increasingly mainstream. Right-wing politicians and media outlets regularly argue that supporters of Palestinian rights, Black Lives Matter, or climate protestors are not just naïve or misguided, they are aiding terrorism. Protest becomes sabotage. Dissent becomes treason.

This erosion of moral clarity serves a strategic purpose. If there are no innocents, then all force is justified. If entire populations can be lumped together as a threat, then mass punishment becomes legitimate. It is not just about war, it is about reframing justice, ethics, and even reality.

One might ask how different this is from the logic of actual terrorism. When non-state actors target civilians, they often claim those victims were not truly innocent, that they were part of a system of oppression or colonialism. That same logic is now echoed by state actors who should, by law and morality, know better.

At what point do we admit that the language of terrorism has been so corrupted, so inverted, that it now allows those with the most firepower to claim the most innocence, and those with none to be cast as existential threats?

If a government can declare an entire people complicit, then the question becomes not who is a terrorist, but who is safe from being labelled one.

## Section 6: - The Myth of the Apolitical Victim – Silence as Guilt

In the modern era of asymmetrical warfare and politicised violence, a deeply unsettling narrative has emerged: the idea that silence is itself a form of guilt. That to be neutral is to be complicit. That if you do not loudly condemn terrorism, then you must support it. This logic, pervasive in state discourse, media commentary, and social media outrage, strips away the possibility of civilian innocence in contested zones.

This is particularly evident in the Israeli-Palestinian conflict, where civilians in Gaza are often presumed guilty by default. Israel's government has frequently argued that Hamas is "deeply embedded in the population" and that the people of Gaza voted for Hamas in 2006, thereby making them complicit in its actions. The election, nearly two decades ago, has been used as a retroactive justification for civilian deaths, as if a ballot cast in a fractured and externally manipulated democratic process renders every future child a legitimate target.

But the logic does not stop there. Israeli Defence Minister Yoav Gallant declared during the 2023 siege of Gaza that "we are fighting human animals." Such dehumanising language primes domestic and international audiences to believe that anything that follows is justified. A school bombed? A hospital destroyed? A bakery flattened? It does not matter, because the people inside did not rise up against Hamas. Their silence becomes proof of sympathy.

Yet what choice do these people have? In authoritarian or militarised regimes, speaking out is often a death sentence. To demand that every civilian oppose a ruling power or face reclassification as an enemy is not just unrealistic, it is inhumane.

We saw this same doctrine applied in the U.S. "War on Terror." In Afghanistan, the Taliban's grip on large swathes of rural territory was used to justify bombing campaigns on entire villages. U.S. spokespeople routinely described these regions as Taliban "strongholds," even when the population had no power to resist. If a drone strike killed a wedding party, the immediate assumption was that militants were among them, or that the villagers were "harbouring" them. The very absence of resistance became evidence of guilt.

This presumption infects domestic politics too. In 2020, then-President Donald Trump labelled Black Lives Matter as a terrorist organisation. Protestors were branded "thugs," "anarchists," and "anti-American." The implication was clear: if you marched for justice, you were part of a violent conspiracy. If you stayed silent, you were still suspect. Either way, the space for innocence vanished.

British authorities have similarly blurred these lines. The arrest of Palestine Action protestors, including clergy members and a 91-year-old woman, under terrorism laws suggests that peaceful civil disobedience can now be redefined as extremist. Those who did not loudly condemn the protests, or who sympathised with the cause but not the methods, were warned that they were treading dangerously close to supporting terrorism. The line between political speech and criminal complicity is no longer legal, it is ideological.

This ideological weaponisation of silence is not just dangerous, it is corrosive to democracy. It creates a world in which citizens are forced into performative condemnation, compelled to denounce enemies of the state to prove their own innocence. And, as with all authoritarian logics, the list of enemies is ever-expanding.

The core problem lies in the binary: you are either with us or against us. In this framework, there is no room for nuance, complexity, or quiet resistance. There is no room for fear, survival, or trauma. Silence is not understood as a protective mechanism, but as a political stance. And political stances must be punished.

When silence becomes guilt, everyone becomes a potential terrorist. And when that happens, the war on terrorism is no longer about stopping violence, it is about enforcing conformity.

## Section 7: - When Everyone's a Suspect – The Expansion of Guilt

In the age of modern counter-terrorism, the scope of suspicion has widened to such an extent that it now threatens to engulf entire populations. What began as a targeted strategy to disrupt violent non-state actors has morphed into a pervasive doctrine of collective culpability, where identity, geography, ideology, or even association can place one under the shadow of suspicion.

This is how "terrorism" has become not just a label for individuals who commit violence, but a net thrown over families, communities, and even nations. It is why Palestinians are often assumed guilty by birthright. It is why Uyghur Muslims in China are interned by the hundreds of thousands in the name of "preventing extremism." It is why Rohingya refugees fleeing Myanmar were portrayed as a threat rather than victims of genocide. The state, in each case, casts itself as the guardian of civilisation, and those on the receiving end of its violence are not viewed as civilians, but as latent terrorists.

Nowhere is this more evident than in the language of "sympathisers," a term that allows for the persecution of those who may never have picked up a weapon, but whose silence, suffering, or shared identity is treated as incriminating. Politicians have fuelled this dynamic. In Northern Ireland, during the height of The Troubles, unionist leaders often suggested that Catholic communities were turning a blind eye to IRA violence. Entire neighbourhoods were treated as if they were breeding grounds for terror, paving the way for sweeping military actions under the Special Powers Act, a law that effectively suspended civil liberties in the name of security.

In the United States, Republican lawmakers and media personalities repeatedly suggested that Muslim communities were "not doing enough" to root out extremism. This vague, unmeasurable burden served to legitimise surveillance, mosque infiltration, and the infamous No-Fly Lists. A similar logic was used to justify Trump's travel ban on citizens from majority-Muslim countries, not because of anything they had done, but because of what they might do, someday, somewhere.

And in Israel, the idea that the entire population of Gaza bears moral responsibility for Hamas has allowed for the erosion of civilian protections. The state narrative is that every civilian is either a human shield or a terrorist in waiting. There is no space for innocence. This is not counter-terrorism, it is pre-emptive collective punishment, cloaked in legal language and defended as "security."

This expansion of guilt has legal implications too. In many jurisdictions, "material support for terrorism" laws are now so broadly defined that donating to a charity accused of tangential links to a proscribed group can land someone in prison. The distinction between intention and association has collapsed. In some cases, even attending a protest, if the government labels it as linked to extremism, can result in arrest under anti-terror laws. The net is now cast so wide that it traps not just perpetrators, but bystanders, advocates, and critics alike.

This tactic serves two purposes. First, it creates a chilling effect, discouraging people from expressing dissent, engaging in activism, or even expressing sympathy for those caught in war zones. Second, it provides governments with near-total narrative control. If everyone is a suspect, then no one is innocent. And if no one is innocent, then there is no injustice, only necessary force.

We must ask: where does this lead?

If entire communities are criminalised by proximity to perceived terrorists, then state violence becomes not only permissible, but expected. We drift into a world where surveillance becomes default, where civil liberties are curtailed not for what you have done, but for who you are or who you know. It is a world in which democracy wears the mask of security, and liberty is sacrificed on the altar of fear.

And yet, this is not the world of some dystopian fiction, it is the world we are living in. It is the terrain on which modern terrorism discourse plays out. And until we confront the ways in which guilt is assigned, suspicion is racialised, and power is protected through the mass criminalisation of "the other," we will never escape the cycle of violence that the war on terror has helped to entrench.

# CHAPTER TEN

## Section 1: - The Weaponisation of Protest

There was a time when protest was considered a democratic right, perhaps even a democratic duty. In the wake of injustice, people marched, rallied, sat in, and shouted out. They occupied town squares and city halls, chained themselves to gates, and held placards aloft in defiance of war, oppression, corruption, or inequality. That was protest. That was democracy in action.

But in the 21st century, a chilling transformation has occurred. What was once a proud expression of civic engagement has become, in the eyes of many governments, a threat, a risk, a crime. In some cases, even an act of terrorism.

We are now firmly in the era of criminalised dissent, where raising your voice too loudly, in the wrong place, or about the wrong issue can see you branded as a subversive, a radical, or worse. Protest is being reframed not as a pressure valve for democratic societies, but as a security concern. And when the state labels something a security concern, the full arsenal of surveillance, control, and suppression comes into play.

Consider the case of Palestine Action in the UK, a direct-action network targeting companies profiting from Israeli military violence, including arms manufacturer Elbit Systems. Protesters scaled buildings, blocked entrances, and sprayed red paint to symbolise blood. Disruptive? Certainly. Illegal? Often, yes. But terrorism? That is the label some British authorities have sought to apply. In 2023, several elderly members of the group, including a 91-year-old nun, priests, and long-retired peace activists, were arrested under suspicion of supporting or facilitating terrorist activity.

The message was clear: it is not just violent radicals who risk being caught in the net of counterterrorism law. Peaceful dissenters, religious activists, and symbolic protesters can also be ensnared if they target the wrong interests. The phrase "support for terrorism" is now so elastic it can stretch to fit nuns with placards and pastors with megaphones.

The same trend is evident across the Atlantic. During the height of the Black Lives Matter (BLM) protests in 2020, then-President Donald Trump routinely described protesters as "terrorists," "anarchists," and "thugs." He claimed, without evidence, that Antifa, short for "anti-fascist," was a domestic terror group. There were calls from right-wing politicians to label BLM itself as a terrorist organisation. Never mind the cause—police brutality, racial injustice, state-sanctioned violence. The protest was rebranded as the threat. The protesters, as enemies.

It did not stop there. In cities across the United States, heavily militarised police responded to peaceful protests with rubber bullets, tear gas, and mass arrests. Journalists were detained. Medics were assaulted. Ordinary citizens were kettled, surveilled, and monitored. Entire movements, mobilised in grief and anger at the state-sanctioned killings of Black Americans, were framed as terrorist-adjacent threats to law and order.

That framing matters. Because once dissent is reframed as extremism, any response is justified. Excessive force becomes precautionary. Pre-trial detention becomes prudent. Surveillance becomes "public safety." And the protesters themselves? They become enemies of the state.

This is the dark genius of terrorism laws. They create a space where ordinary laws no longer apply. Once the word "terrorism" enters the picture, democratic norms are suspended. Due process weakens. The presumption of innocence fades. And the state is permitted to act in ways it otherwise could not. That is why governments are so eager to use the term, because it changes the rules of the game.

And it is not just the protesters who are criminalised. It is those who stand beside them. Guilt by association is a core tactic. Attend a protest where someone throws a stone? You might be labelled an extremist. Retweet a video showing a sit-in at an arms factory? You might be accused of supporting terrorism. This slippery slope ends not in justice, but in fear and self-censorship.

At its core, this is not about stopping violence. It is about stopping resistance. It is about redefining dissent as danger, and protest as provocation. And once that shift takes hold, democracy begins to suffocate under the weight of its own security state.

## Section 2: How States Manufacture Extremists

The irony at the heart of counterterrorism is this: the more a state suppresses legitimate protest, the more likely it is to radicalise the very people it seeks to silence.

This phenomenon is not new. History is littered with movements that began peacefully and became radicalised only after facing brutal crackdowns. But in today's world, where dissent is conflated with danger, the process is accelerating. States, by their actions, are manufacturing extremists.

To understand this dynamic, we must recognise the emotional and psychological arc of protest. Most people do not begin their political engagement by throwing Molotov cocktails or joining armed cells. They start with a grievance. A belief that something is wrong. A cause worth fighting for. They write letters. They sign petitions. They attend marches. They shout slogans and carry signs. These are acts of faith in the system, the belief that if enough people speak, those in power might listen.

But what happens when those protests are ignored? What happens when peaceful demonstrations are met with tear gas, arrests, or accusations of terrorism? The message is clear: your voice does not matter. Your grievance will not be addressed. And if you keep pushing, you will be punished.

That is the moment radicalisation begins.

Take the case of Kashmir, where decades of military occupation and political exclusion by the Indian state have turned generations of disaffected youth into militants. The Indian government routinely brands all forms of resistance in Kashmir as terrorism, even when it is peaceful. Protests are banned. Internet access is cut. Community leaders are jailed. In this vacuum of rights, anger festers. And some turn to violence not because they began there, but because the path to peaceful change was systematically closed off.

Or consider Palestinian youth in the West Bank. Many have lived their entire lives under occupation, checkpoints, and the constant threat of home demolition. When they throw stones, they are called terrorists. When they protest, they are arrested. When they post on social media, they are surveilled. Every avenue of non-violent expression is criminalised. What is left? The state, in its suppression, radicalises its subjects and then uses their radicalisation to justify even harsher crackdowns.

This is the paradox of authoritarian counterterrorism: the more brutal the state becomes, the more it produces the very extremism it claims to oppose. It is not just that repression fails, it is that it creates the conditions for violent resistance.

In France, this cycle has played out in the suburbs, banlieues, where disillusioned young Muslims face systemic discrimination, police profiling, and economic exclusion. After terrorist attacks on French soil, entire communities are treated as suspect. Mosques are raided. Surveillance is increased. Hate crimes spike. And when marginalised youth respond with anger, they are cast as proof of the state's original suspicion. The snake swallows its tail.

In the United States, the post-9/11 surveillance of Muslim communities turned neighbourhoods into open-air intelligence zones. Religious leaders were monitored. Youth were interrogated. Community centres were infiltrated. The state justified these actions by claiming they were preventing radicalisation. But what they actually did was breed resentment, suspicion, and alienation. As countless security experts have since warned, you cannot police your way out of extremism. You must address the underlying grievances that fuel it.

And what are those grievances? Political exclusion. State violence. Racism. Inequality. Injustice. These are not terrorist ideologies. They are political conditions. And when the only response a state offers is suppression, people inevitably seek other means.

The sociologist Marc Sageman, a former CIA officer who studied jihadist movements, once noted that the majority of people who turn to political violence are not mentally ill, ideologically driven fanatics, but normal individuals who reached a breaking point. "It is not the ideology," he argued, "it is the sense of injustice."

This sense of injustice is what transforms protesters into radicals. When the system is unresponsive, when peaceful resistance is punished, when every avenue is closed, desperation grows. And with it, the appeal of more confrontational tactics.

So when we ask, "Why do they hate us?" or "Why are they turning to violence?" we should first ask, "What did we do to make them feel they had no other choice?"

Extremism is not born in a vacuum. It is often forged in the crucible of state repression. And if governments truly want to prevent radicalisation, they must first stop creating the conditions for it.

## Section 3: The Surveillance State and the Silencing of Dissent

Surveillance is no longer just a tool of intelligence gathering; it is a mechanism of social control. In the name of security, states across the world have constructed vast digital and physical infrastructures to watch, record, and predict the behaviours of their citizens. But far from just targeting terrorists, this machinery is now aimed at everyone, especially those who dissent.

The modern surveillance state was turbocharged by 9/11, but it has since outgrown its original purpose. What began as a counter-terrorism strategy has metastasised into an all-encompassing system of monitoring, profiling, and controlling populations. In the name of preventing future attacks, governments have normalised the collection of metadata, the scanning of private messages, the tracking of geolocation, and the facial recognition of protesters. In this digital panopticon, everyone is a suspect. Every protester is a potential threat.

Edward Snowden's 2013 revelations exposed the true extent of the National Security Agency (NSA)'s surveillance operations, not just of foreign enemies, but of American citizens. Millions of people had their phone records, emails, and online activity swept up in secret programmes authorised by secret courts, under laws few had read. All in the name of preventing terrorism.

But the scope of surveillance soon shifted. It was not just "terrorists" being tracked; it was activists. Journalists. Whistleblowers. Environmental campaigners. Black Lives Matter organisers. In the United Kingdom, peaceful campaigners from groups like Extinction Rebellion were placed on counter-terror watchlists. In the United States, the FBI's COINTELPRO legacy was reborn through the monitoring of racial justice movements. Law enforcement agencies built dossiers on protest leaders, used social media scraping tools to identify "agitators," and even deployed undercover officers to infiltrate legal demonstrations.

The implications are chilling. When people know they are being watched, they self-censor. They avoid protests. They stop speaking openly. They hesitate to criticise the state. This is not just surveillance; it is suppression. The goal is not just to monitor dissent, but to discourage it.

And it works.

The "chilling effect" of surveillance is well documented. A 2016 study by PEN America found that writers in the United States were altering or avoiding certain topics for fear of government monitoring. Others avoided visiting websites or engaging with politically sensitive content online. Free speech, in this context, becomes a performance, one shaped by fear, not freedom.

Surveillance also disproportionately targets marginalised communities. Muslim populations in Europe and North America, for example, are vastly overrepresented in government monitoring programmes. In France, the "Prevent" strategy was used to track Muslim schoolchildren for signs of radicalisation. In the UK, the Prevent duty imposed on teachers and doctors turned civil society actors into intelligence gatherers, flagging students for political views, religious clothing, or even dissatisfaction with foreign policy. These programmes were not about catching terrorists; they were about creating a culture of suspicion, especially around dissenting views.

In authoritarian regimes, the surveillance state is even more aggressive. In China, the Social Credit System and expansive facial recognition networks allow the government to track, reward, or punish citizens for behaviours deemed acceptable or subversive. In Russia, laws framed as anti-extremism are used to monitor critics of the state, particularly those opposing the war in Ukraine. In Iran, surveillance is fused with morality policing, used to detain women for dress code violations or digital activists for questioning the regime.

Yet the line between authoritarian and democratic practices is blurring. Western governments now routinely adopt the tools and justifications of authoritarian states, citing national security as the ultimate trump card. This convergence poses a dangerous question: what happens when the tools of tyranny are normalised in democracies?

It is here that we must confront the false binary between safety and freedom. Governments argue that surveillance is necessary to keep us safe. But safe from what, and for whom? If the cost of safety is silence, if security requires the death of dissent, then what kind of society are we protecting?

Surveillance, in this context, is not neutral. It is selective. Strategic. Political. It does not just watch terrorists; it watches those who challenge the narrative of power. And in doing so, it becomes a weapon, not of protection, but of pre-emption. Not of justice, but of intimidation.

When people fear the state more than the terrorist, the war on terror has already been lost.

## Section 4: When the Centre Cannot Hold – The Collapse of Trust

The great paradox of the War on Terror is that, in the name of protecting democratic societies, it has often undermined the very foundations that make those societies democratic. Nowhere is this more visible than in the erosion of public trust. Trust in institutions. Trust in leadership. Trust in truth itself.

In the years following 9/11, Western governments asked their citizens to accept extraordinary measures: surveillance, censorship, black sites, pre-emptive wars. Each was sold as temporary, targeted, and necessary. But as the years dragged on, and the terror threats shifted, morphed, or disappeared altogether, those measures remained. Worse, they were expanded. Powers granted to fight terrorism were retooled to fight dissent. Police budgets swelled. Civil liberties shrank. And trust, once the glue of democratic governance, began to decay.

When people no longer believe in the good faith of their governments, everything begins to unravel. They question the motives behind policy. They doubt the integrity of elections. They turn away from mainstream media, dismissing it as propaganda. They see public institutions not as protectors, but as predators.

This crisis of trust is not an accident. It is the predictable result of years of state overreach, official hypocrisy, and double standards. Governments that justify civilian deaths in the Middle East as collateral damage cannot expect moral authority at home. Leaders who defend indefinite detention without trial cannot credibly speak of due process. States that label every critic a threat cannot convincingly champion free speech. The moral high ground erodes when it is built on contradictions.

The rise of alternative media and conspiracy movements is not simply the fault of algorithms or Facebook echo chambers. It is a symptom of institutional failure. When truth is bent to serve the state, when official narratives obscure more than they reveal, people will seek other sources, however flawed. The problem is not just misinformation. It is disinformation by omission—the stories that are never told, the crimes that are never acknowledged, the lives that are never mourned because they died on the wrong side of the narrative.

Nowhere is this collapse more visible than in younger generations. Polls across the West show plummeting confidence in democratic institutions. In the United States, less than half of young adults believe that democracy is essential. In the UK, a significant number of young voters express support for authoritarian alternatives if they can deliver results. Around the world, apathy is giving way to anger and anger, increasingly, to alienation.

This breakdown of trust creates fertile ground for populists and strongmen. They thrive on institutional failure. They weaponise it. They promise to burn it all down and for many, that sounds like justice. After years of being ignored, surveilled, or lied to, people are not looking for polished politicians. They are looking for someone who will break the system, even if that person is dangerous, even if they do not believe in democracy. Because when democracy no longer delivers justice, even its defenders begin to waver.

Trust, once lost, is hard to rebuild. It requires more than reforms or apologies. It requires a reckoning, a genuine confrontation with the failures of the post-9/11 era. The lies that led to war. The silence around torture. The erosion of rights in the name of security. The deaths that were never counted, the guilt that was never admitted.

This book is not a call for cynicism. It is a call for clarity. We cannot fix what we refuse to name. And we cannot restore trust until we admit how, and why, it was broken.

Because when the centre cannot hold, as Yeats warned, "things fall apart." And in the rubble, the only voices left standing may be those who were once pushed to the margins, the ones dismissed, surveilled, or silenced as dangerous.

Sometimes, they were.

But sometimes, they were right.

## Section 5: Dehumanisation and the Language of Security

At the heart of modern counter-terrorism lies a carefully constructed linguistic shield, a vocabulary designed not to explain, but to obscure. It is the language of national security, and its most enduring function is to dehumanise. Once a person or group is labelled a threat, they cease to be individuals with histories, grievances, or families. They become targets, statistics, or shadows. And in that shift, a thousand crimes can be justified.

Dehumanisation is not new. Every war has relied on it. But in the post-9/11 world, it was industrialised. Muslims became "radicalised." Civilians became "human shields." Whole cities were described as "terrorist strongholds." And once this vocabulary took root, the killing became easier, easier to do and easier to forget.

A drone strike does not kill Fatima and her three children. It "neutralises high-value targets." A bombing campaign does not incinerate a wedding party. It "removes insurgents." The bodies pulled from the rubble are not daughters, brothers, grandmothers, they are "collateral damage." Language becomes armour. Words deflect the moral weight of violence. Bureaucrats can sign death warrants without a flicker of guilt, because those they kill have already been rendered faceless.

This is why terms like "enemy combatant," "unlawful belligerent," or "terror-affiliated area" matter. They are not descriptors. They are permissions. They allow states to act without consequence, to violate laws, to bypass conscience. Because once the people on the receiving end are no longer seen as fully human, the full spectrum of cruelty becomes available. Torture becomes "enhanced interrogation." Indefinite detention becomes "security necessity." Assassination becomes "targeted killing."

This linguistic framework does not just mask state violence, it recalibrates public perception. Polls show that when civilians in Gaza or Iraq are described as "suspected militants" or "terror-adjacent," Western audiences are significantly less likely to express concern over their deaths, even if no evidence is ever provided. The suggestion alone is enough. It primes the reader, the viewer, the voter. These people do not deserve our empathy. They are dangerous. They brought it on themselves.

Israel's bombardment of Gaza is a masterclass in this technique. When entire apartment blocks are flattened, the IDF spokesperson rarely speaks of dead children or displaced families. The strike was "surgical," the target was "eliminated," the collateral damage "unfortunate." In the process, the scale of the violence is sanitised. The images might show carnage, but the words suggest control, rationality, justice. In fact, the Israeli military has even coined euphemisms like "mowing the lawn" to refer to repeated assaults on Gaza, implying routine maintenance, not mass death.

But this is not unique to Israel. The United States, the UK, France, Russia, and China have all mastered the language of technocratic brutality. Modern military press briefings sound more like corporate risk reports than descriptions of war. There is a quiet, bureaucratic horror in the phrase "acceptable civilian casualty ratio," a kind of madness cloaked in the language of rationality.

The goal is always the same: to prevent the public from seeing and feeling what violence really is. Because if they did, if the mothers crying over dead sons in Mosul, Rafah, or Khartoum were heard in their full humanity, the political cost of endless war might become unbearable. So the voices are silenced, distorted, or buried under terminology so bland, so abstract, that it no longer feels like death at all.

But the dehumanisation does not stop at language. It becomes policy. It shapes who gets rescued and who gets left behind. Which refugees are welcomed and which are turned away. It decides whether a protester is labelled "concerned" or "extremist," whether a community is policed or protected, whether an entire people are granted the dignity of self-defence or denied it outright, as Netanyahu did when asked whether Palestinians had the right to resist. "No," he replied.

To call this mere bias is to understate it. This is the machinery of moral erasure, and it is global.

Undoing it will require more than accurate words. It will require seeing those we have been told to fear as full human beings, not as threats, not as abstractions, not as "others," but as people. As parents, siblings, neighbours. As individuals with names, hopes, and histories. As victims too of the stories we were sold.

Because language does not just describe reality.

It builds it.

## Section 6: - A New Ideological Battlefield

In the 20th century, war was waged on land, sea, and in the skies. In the 21st, a new front has emerged: the battle for ideological control. Here, the weapons are not tanks or drones, but narratives, platforms, and moral claims. It is a war of definitions, fought not just between armies but between ideas. And nowhere is that more visible than in the question of what terrorism is and who gets to define it.

Terrorism today is not just a tactic. It is a label of exclusion. A declaration that the actor in question is not worthy of rights, recognition, or even life. But what makes this battlefield especially dangerous is that it is no longer just states using the label to delegitimise enemies, it is private platforms, media conglomerates, and even algorithms doing the same. A protest flagged by Facebook's moderation system as "extremist." A hashtag banned on X for "terror-related content." A YouTube video of police brutality demonetised or taken down. These are not isolated incidents. They are the new front lines of narrative warfare.

The ideological battlefield is policed by a strange alliance of state interests, corporate incentives, and public paranoia. Tech giants like Meta, Google, and X now have more power than most governments to decide which voices are heard and which are suppressed. They make decisions about what constitutes "hate speech," "radicalisation," or "community safety" with little transparency, driven by vague community guidelines, advertiser pressure, and the fear of regulatory backlash. Governments, meanwhile, exploit this corporate machinery. They nudge platforms behind closed doors, feed them watchlists, and pressure them to act "responsibly." Responsibility, of course, is defined as censorship in the name of security.

But the battlefield is also internal. Within societies. Within ourselves. Citizens are now expected to self-police, to report "suspicious behaviour," to avoid "controversial" topics, to adopt the language of the war on terror as their own. Schools teach "Prevent" programmes. Employers require counter-extremism training. Mosques, community centres, even libraries are expected to act as surveillance nodes. Ideological conformity becomes the norm, not because of open coercion but through the subtle fear of being labelled.

Once a person is branded "sympathetic to terrorism," their life changes. It does not require proof, only association. A shared tweet. A WhatsApp group. A donation to the wrong charity. And suddenly, careers are ended, visas revoked, passports suspended, bank accounts frozen. No trial. No appeal. Just suspicion, amplified by the machinery of ideological control.

This battlefield also targets language itself. Words like "resistance," "intifada," "struggle," or even "Palestine" can trigger moderation flags or algorithmic suppression. Journalists have reported stories being delayed or downranked because they used terminology deemed "sensitive." Academics and artists face cancellation for exploring themes that challenge dominant narratives. Even the phrase "international law" can be treated as subversive, depending on whose actions it critiques.

There is a profound danger in this ideological terrain. Because once the space for contested ideas disappears, so too does democracy. If only one narrative is permitted, then all others, no matter how justified, become heresies. And those who voice them become dissidents, or worse, terrorists.

The Israeli-Palestinian conflict is again illustrative. It is not just a military struggle, it is a narrative war. Israel frames its actions as "self-defence," its critics as "antisemites," and its opponents as "terrorists." Palestinians who resist occupation, whether with stones or slogans, are painted with the same brush. And the platforms that dominate global discourse often reinforce this framing. Videos of Israeli airstrikes are allowed to circulate. Videos of their aftermath, less so.

The ideological battlefield is not fair. It is asymmetric. Those with power, military, economic, or digital, define the rules. And those without are expected to play along or be silenced. The irony is that many of those silenced are precisely the voices that could help build peace: the human rights defenders, the whistle-blowers, the journalists, the survivors.

Yet, despite this, the battle is not lost. Alternative platforms are emerging. Grassroots media, decentralised networks, and encrypted communications offer new ways to challenge dominant narratives. Whistle-blowers like Edward Snowden, journalists like Glenn Greenwald, and activists across the globe continue to expose abuses and amplify dissent. They remind us that while the ideological battlefield is vast and treacherous, it is not unwinnable.

But we must recognise it for what it is. A war for meaning. A fight over who gets to define truth, justice, and terror. And in that war, silence is complicity.

Because in the end, this is not just about terrorism.

It is about the world we want to live in and who gets to shape it.

## Section 7: - Weaponising Fear: The Media as an Enforcer of State Narratives

If dissent is criminalised and protest reframed as extremism, the media plays an essential role as the enforcer of that illusion. In today's interconnected world, mainstream news outlets, online platforms, and social media echo chambers do not just reflect state power, they often amplify and legitimise it. And when it comes to terrorism, the media narrative is not just a story, it is a verdict. The framing of acts of violence, resistance, or even humanitarian advocacy depends less on the facts than on who is doing the framing.

News outlets regularly use loaded language when describing the "enemy" versus the "ally." One man's militant is another's freedom fighter, but one man's insurgent is another's defender of the homeland. The distinction is rarely examined. Western coverage of wars and insurgencies, particularly in the Middle East, reveals this bias. When a Palestinian child is killed in an Israeli airstrike, the headline reads: "Child Dies in Gaza Violence"—passive voice, devoid of accountability. But when an Israeli citizen is killed in a retaliatory attack, the wording changes dramatically: "Terror Attack Kills Israeli Teen." The actor is named, the emotion evoked, the label firmly applied.

This differential language is no accident. It is part of a broader system of manufacturing consent. Noam Chomsky and Edward Herman outlined this dynamic in *Manufacturing Consent*, where media institutions act less as independent watchdogs and more as filters of acceptable discourse. In the War on Terror era, this filtering has become even more pronounced. Coverage of U.S. drone strikes in Yemen or Afghanistan often uses phrases like "suspected militants" or "targeted compounds," while offering little or no evidence, no photographic confirmation, and certainly no post-strike accountability. What is missing from those stories are names, faces, families, and funerals.

Meanwhile, the same media give extensive space to terrorism trials in the West, complete with biographies of victims, expert commentary, and government condemnation. The result is a double lens: one in high definition, the other fogged with euphemism and distance. This lens conditions audiences to accept that state violence is not just justifiable, it is normal, even necessary.

Consider how the term "homegrown terrorist" is weaponised in Western democracies. Often applied to Muslims born in Europe or America, it assumes that these individuals are somehow foreign despite their citizenship. Their motivations are framed as irrational, fanatical, or culturally rooted in "extremism." Rarely is Western foreign policy, economic inequality, or systemic discrimination considered a legitimate cause of radicalisation. When white supremacists carry out attacks, such as in Christchurch, Buffalo, or Oslo, the media often avoids the word "terrorist," opting instead for "shooter," "attacker," or "lone wolf." Their manifestos are examined in psychological terms, not political ones. Their communities are spared collective blame.

This is not simply biased reporting. It is strategic silence in service of power. It shapes who is feared and who is pitied, who is defended and who is expendable.

In this context, social media has become both a threat and an extension of state control. On one hand, platforms like Twitter/X, YouTube, and Facebook have enabled activist voices to bypass traditional media filters, allowing marginalised groups to document human rights abuses, share alternative narratives, and challenge dominant assumptions. On the other hand, these same platforms have become complicit in censorship, surveillance, and deplatforming. Under pressure from governments, tech companies now routinely remove posts deemed "supportive of terrorism" with little due process or clarity. The line between incitement and resistance, reporting and radicalisation, has become dangerously blurred.

For example, Palestinian journalists and activists have reported mass takedowns of accounts that share footage from Gaza or voice criticism of Israeli military actions. In India, Kashmiri activists have faced digital blackouts, account suspensions, and algorithmic suppression. Across Africa and Latin America, civil society groups are routinely labelled as extremist simply for opposing corrupt regimes.

The end result is a media landscape that not only mirrors state ideology but actively enforces it. This is not journalism, it is narrative warfare.

By shaping perception, the media helps build the scaffolding of the terrorist label. It creates the heroes, the villains, and the story arc that lets state violence slip through unexamined. It offers the soothing fiction that terror is always theirs, never ours. And perhaps most powerfully, it turns the public into passive accomplices, willing not only to believe the story, but to repeat it.

## Section 8: - The Psychological Toll: Citizenship in an Age of Suspicion

In an age where terrorism is omnipresent in political discourse, citizenship itself has become conditional. The shadow of suspicion now hangs over entire communities, often based on race, religion, or nationality, not individual conduct. The psychological toll of this suspicion is profound, and it runs deeper than the physical consequences of violence. It erodes belonging. It fractures identity. It tells people, in subtle and not-so-subtle ways: You are here, but you are not one of us.

For many Muslims in the West, this has become an everyday reality. They are watched, questioned, searched, monitored, online and in public. Ordinary acts like attending a mosque, travelling abroad, growing a beard, or wearing a hijab are all enough to trigger scrutiny. The premise is not guilt by action but suspicion by association. One can be born in a country, pay taxes, vote, and still be viewed as a latent threat. Their very citizenship is seen as provisional, always subject to reevaluation in times of crisis.

This creates a psychic burden that is rarely acknowledged in counterterrorism policy debates. It is the burden of having to prove your loyalty, to be the "good Muslim," to denounce acts you never committed, to be held accountable for violence you do not support. And this dynamic does not stop with Muslims. Any community that challenges the state narrative, from Indigenous protesters to anti-war activists, finds itself in a similar bind. The question becomes not what have you done, but who are you and what do you represent?

This is how fear is nationalised. The state tells its citizens: "We will protect you from them," and in doing so divides the population into protected and suspected. The "them" could be brown, Black, Arab, leftist, poor, foreign, non-Christian, it does not matter. What matters is that the line is drawn. Once it is, the machinery of suspicion takes over. Background checks, border screenings, surveillance dragnets, algorithmic profiling—all these become normalised, and resistance becomes dangerous.

The irony, of course, is that this paranoia does not make societies safer. In fact, it creates the conditions in which alienation, resentment, and marginalisation flourish. It delegitimises voices that could offer insight or solutions. It breeds silence and shame. In some cases, it radicalises the very people it seeks to pacify.

Former Guantánamo detainees have spoken of the crushing impact of indefinite detention without trial, years lost, families destroyed, identities erased. Even after their release, they are haunted by stigma. One man, Moazzam Begg, who was never charged with a crime, described the post-release years as another kind of imprisonment: "You are free, but only in name. You are not free in the eyes of your neighbours, your employer, or your government." His story is not an anomaly. It is the logical conclusion of a system that punishes people not for what they have done, but for what they could be.

In this context, the word "citizen" loses its protective power. It becomes hollow. A badge of privilege for some and a licence of scrutiny for others. And as citizenship becomes weaponised, redefined by race, loyalty, and compliance, democracy begins to erode. Not in a dramatic coup, but in a quiet surrender to fear.

Surveillance becomes virtue. Dissent becomes disloyalty. And terrorism becomes not a tactic or a crime, but a floating label, ready to be applied to whoever the state needs to silence next.

# CHAPTER ELEVEN:
## Authoritarian by Design

## Section 1: How the Erosion of Trust and the Centralisation of Power Make Strongmen Inevitable

In a functioning democracy, trust is the lifeblood of the system, trust in institutions, in the rule of law, in the press, in public services, in the idea that accountability still matters. When that trust erodes, something far more dangerous moves in to fill the vacuum: the craving for control.

It rarely begins with a dictator. It begins with a loss of faith. A sense that the system is broken, that "the elites" are playing by different rules, that your vote does not count, that corruption is everywhere. And this feeling, exploited by opportunists, is what opens the door for the rise of authoritarianism.

Across the democratic world, we have witnessed this trend accelerate. Leaders once elected on promises of reform become increasingly intolerant of scrutiny. Parliaments are sidelined. Independent media are branded as enemies. Civil servants are purged. The judiciary is packed with loyalists. Protests are suppressed, not with open violence at first, but with creeping legislation. The architecture of democracy is left standing, but hollowed from within.

The tools of counter-terrorism are frequently used to enable this shift. Emergency powers introduced in response to genuine threats are never fully repealed. Surveillance infrastructures built for national security are redirected inward, against journalists, activists, and dissenters. The language of patriotism is weaponised, and those who raise concerns are labelled unpatriotic, ungrateful, or worse, terrorist sympathisers.

It is no accident that countries sliding into authoritarianism often cite terrorism as justification. Viktor Orbán in Hungary declared a state of emergency over migration, calling it a "security threat." Turkey's President Erdoğan used the failed 2016 coup attempt to launch a purge of over 100,000 civil servants and journalists under the guise of rooting out terrorism. In India, Narendra Modi's government has used anti-terror laws to detain student protesters and critics of Hindu nationalism. The same pattern plays out in Israel, where those questioning the war in Gaza face intimidation, job loss, or arrest under terrorism-related charges.

And in the United States, Donald Trump's presidency offered a blueprint. He labelled Antifa a terrorist organisation, despite it not being an organisation, called Black Lives Matter a threat to public order, and declared journalists to be "the enemy of the people." His administration toyed with invoking the Insurrection Act against protesters, deployed federal agents without identification to suppress demonstrations, and floated the idea of deploying military force on American streets.

The dangerous irony is this: the more authoritarian a state becomes, the more it insists it is defending democracy. It wraps repression in the flag, paints opposition as chaos, and reframes its power grab as "order." This is what makes strongmen not only possible but popular. In moments of insecurity, many people will trade liberty for safety, especially when that liberty seems increasingly inaccessible to them anyway.

And the legal scaffolding is often already in place. Counter-terror legislation, with its vague definitions and broad powers, becomes the perfect tool for authoritarian consolidation. Laws that allow for indefinite detention, expanded surveillance, or the banning of organisations are no longer hypothetical, they are active levers of power, waiting for someone to pull.

This does not happen in the shadows. It happens in plain sight. It is announced at press conferences, justified in parliament, and echoed on mainstream media. It is approved by frightened citizens and emboldened by loyal political operatives. And once a society starts down this path, it becomes harder and harder to turn back.

Because strongmen do not simply take power. They are invited in by a public tired of failure, hungry for security, and convinced that the old rules no longer work.

And once inside, they rewrite those rules to ensure they never leave.

## Section 2: - The Expansion of the Label

In the modern security state, the term "terrorist" no longer stops at the person who commits the act. It stretches, absorbs, and metastasises, touching family members, political allies, sympathisers, entire ethnic groups, and entire regions. The result is not merely guilt by association. It is guilt by identity, guilt by opinion, guilt by presence.

Nowhere is this more apparent than in the post-9/11 world, where Western governments have constructed legal frameworks to classify individuals as "supporters of terrorism" not based on actions, but on affiliations, ideology, or even expression. You do not need to carry out an attack. You do not even need to plan one. You just need to appear sympathetic.

In the United States, "material support" laws have been used to convict individuals not for what they did, but for who they communicated with. In 2010, the Supreme Court ruled in *Holder v. Humanitarian Law Project* that even offering non-violent conflict resolution training to a proscribed group constituted material support to terrorism. As Justice Stephen Breyer wrote in dissent, it criminalised "speech advocating the use of peaceful means to achieve political ends." But the majority opinion held, broadening the net of what constitutes terrorism.

In the UK, police have arrested Palestine Action protesters, environmental activists, and even elderly clergymen under terrorism provisions. In one case, a 91-year-old nun was detained for allegedly aiding "terrorist activities" by protesting an arms manufacturer supplying Israel. These were not violent people. They were not plotting attacks. But they opposed the status quo, and in the age of securitised paranoia, that is enough.

## Section 3: The 'No Innocents' Doctrine

One of the most disturbing trends in the weaponisation of the terrorism label is the growing acceptance of the idea that there are no innocents. This philosophy, once the preserve of extremist groups, is now echoed, sometimes subtly and sometimes explicitly, by state actors who seek to justify indiscriminate violence.

Take, for example, the rhetoric surrounding Gaza. In recent conflicts, Israeli officials have increasingly implied that civilians who remain in areas targeted by military strikes are complicit. Prime Minister Benjamin Netanyahu's allies and members of his cabinet have suggested that those who vote for Hamas, or who do not evacuate, are legitimate targets. In 2023, former Israeli Defence Minister Avigdor Lieberman stated, "There are no innocents in Gaza," and urged for the area to be flattened. This chilling logic makes terrorism a demographic, not just an act.

It is not unique to Israel. In the U.S. War on Terror, drone strike policy under both Republican and Democratic administrations employed a "guilt until proven innocent" model. According to documents published by *The Intercept* and statements by former Obama-era officials, all "military-age males" in strike zones were by default considered combatants unless posthumously proven otherwise. The assumption of innocence no longer applied.

This approach is not a quirk of military pragmatism. It is an ideology, a worldview in which whole populations can be branded as suspect. Children become "human shields." Families become "terrorist sympathisers." Every funeral, wedding, or school bombed is reframed as a regrettable but necessary part of the war against terror.

The doctrine of "no innocents" is the ultimate narrative weapon. It absolves the powerful of accountability. It blurs the moral lines. It ensures that the public, fed on fear and security rhetoric, does not ask too many questions about who dies and why.

Contrast this. In Northern Ireland, the PSNI monitors loyalist parades in which the UDA, a well-documented paramilitary organisation responsible for dozens of murders and bombings, is allowed to march in many cases without arrests simply for participation. Meanwhile, in Britain, the state deploys terrorism laws to arrest hundreds of peaceful protesters for carrying placards or shouting slogans in support of Palestine Action, a group whose activities were non-violent, symbolic, and aimed at disrupting arms supply chains, yet whose supporters faced arrests under the Terrorism Act. What this clearly demonstrates is not the consistent application of anti-terror laws but their selectivity. As we have seen time and again, the term "terrorist" is not defined by violence alone, often not by violence at all, but by who uses it, against whom, and why.

The result is a surreal paradox. A group historically linked to lethal paramilitary violence marches with minimal action, while non-violent civil protest becomes a crime subject to the full weight of terrorism legislation. The label of "terrorist" thus becomes untethered from the behaviour it is meant to describe and instead becomes a tool of state power, protest suppression, and narrative control.

## Section 4: Labelling from the Outside – When Empathy Becomes a Threat

In the age of global communication and social media, the power to label does not rest solely with governments. Public solidarity movements, journalists, artists, and everyday citizens have increasingly challenged dominant narratives about who is a terrorist and who is a victim. But in doing so, many have found themselves accused of supporting terrorism simply for showing empathy.

Consider the reaction to international protests in support of Palestinians in Gaza. Demonstrations across Western capitals in 2023 and 2024 were described by prominent political figures as "pro-terrorist rallies." Media outlets ran headlines suggesting that waving a Palestinian flag was tantamount to condoning Hamas. In France, the government pre-emptively banned pro-Palestine protests, citing national security concerns. In Germany, people faced arrest for carrying placards that referenced Palestinian suffering. The implication was clear: to express grief or anger about state violence is to side with terrorists.

The same logic has been applied to those who supported Black Lives Matter, Extinction Rebellion, or even anti-war protests during the invasions of Iraq and Afghanistan. In each case, expressions of dissent were rebranded as dangerous subversion. If you challenge the state's definition of terrorism, you risk becoming a suspect yourself.

Even humanitarian actors are not safe. Aid organisations operating in Gaza, Yemen, or Afghanistan have had their funding cut or been placed under investigation simply because they operated in proximity to groups the West had designated as terrorist organisations. As a result, providing food, shelter, or medical care becomes politicised and punishable.

This dynamic reflects a deeper truth. Empathy threatens the architecture of control. If people begin to see the "enemy" as human, the simplistic moral binary collapses. The myth of the terrorist as evil incarnate requires emotional distance. It cannot survive the sight of a weeping mother, a wounded child, or a desperate refugee pleading for life.

The narrative must be policed, and those who step outside it, those who question, mourn, or refuse to dehumanise, must be silenced, or at least discredited.

That is how labelling works in the modern world. It does not just destroy the lives of those branded as terrorists. It erodes the space for compassion, corrodes the moral imagination, and leaves us with a society in which silence is safe and solidarity is suspect.

## Section 5: The Weaponisation of Guilt by Association

In the age of counterterrorism, guilt is no longer tethered to action. It is increasingly determined by association. To know a "terrorist," to speak to one, to quote their words, to sympathise with their cause, even if you reject their methods, is enough to place yourself under suspicion.

This is not an accident. It is strategy.

Western security agencies have for decades expanded the definition of terrorist activity to include not only acts of violence but "support," "promotion," or "facilitation." These terms are so loosely defined that they allow sweeping surveillance and prosecution of individuals who have never committed, or even advocated, violence. They might be relatives. Friends. Lawyers. Clerics. Academics. Journalists.

We have seen this tactic used in the "War on Terror" against Muslims globally. Parents whose sons travelled to Syria to join ISIS found themselves interrogated, not only for what they may have known, but for what they should have known. Entire communities were placed under surveillance based on mosque attendance, social media shares, or charity donations. Civil liberties were sacrificed on the altar of pre-emptive justice.

But the tactic does not stop with Muslims.

Environmental campaigners have been painted as part of extremist cells. Protesters who chain themselves to machinery are grouped with saboteurs. A grandmother who sends food to a refugee camp can be accused of supporting a terrorist organisation if one of its residents is blacklisted. In Israel, citizens who call for a ceasefire or equal rights for Palestinians are branded "traitors" or "terror sympathisers." In authoritarian states, this guilt-by-association logic is used to justify disappearances, torture, and imprisonment.

This is where the terrorism label becomes most dangerous, when it creeps beyond the violent actor to ensnare those who merely understand, who advocate for root causes, or who refuse to parrot official lines.

When U.S. Congresswoman Ilhan Omar suggested that U.S. foreign policy had contributed to instability in the Middle East, she was accused of defending terrorists. When UK Labour MP Jeremy Corbyn advocated for dialogue with Hamas and Hezbollah as part of a peace strategy, it was cited years later to discredit his leadership, suggesting he had "shared platforms with terrorists." The aim was not to debate his policy. It was to delegitimise him through proximity.

And so, the terrorism narrative functions not just as a weapon against the violent, but as a dragnet for all dissent. It allows governments to shrink the space for critical thinking, debate, or political empathy. It turns speech into crime, contact into complicity, and solidarity into sedition.

The real danger is that this logic is being normalised. In many democratic societies, the presumption of innocence has been quietly reversed. People are forced to prove they do not support terrorism, a standard that is impossible to meet when definitions are fluid, secretive, and politically driven.

As the Israeli journalist Gideon Levy once warned, "When your enemy has no rights, you have no obligations." Guilt by association is the mechanism by which this dehumanisation spreads, from the battlefield to the courtroom, from the activist to the journalist, and finally, to the hearts of an apathetic public.

Because once we accept that people can be punished not for what they do, but for who they know, believe, or mourn, then the war on terrorism is no longer about security. It is about control.

## Section 6: Sympathy as Subversion – The New Thought crime

There was a time when sympathy was seen as a virtue, a human impulse that underpinned empathy, morality, and even diplomacy. But in the post-9/11 world, sympathy has become suspect. Not sympathy for victims of terror, that remains politically correct and publicly encouraged, but sympathy for those labelled terrorists, or for the people and causes associated with them. That, increasingly, is viewed as subversive, dangerous, even criminal.

The rise of what we might call the sympathy crime is not just about what one does or says. It is about how one feels, or is perceived to feel. In this climate, even understanding a "terrorist" becomes treasonous. Asking why someone joined Hamas, the IRA, or the Tamil Tigers is treated as a form of moral weakness or dangerous justification. Exploring context is painted as making excuses.

This is how entire peoples are dehumanised.

Take the Gaza Strip. In 2023–25, as tens of thousands of Palestinians were killed under Israeli bombardment, many of them women and children, global demonstrations erupted in solidarity. Yet protesters carrying "Free Palestine" signs or waving Palestinian flags were routinely accused of supporting terrorism. Even Jewish groups advocating a ceasefire were targeted. In Germany, France, and the UK, protests were banned, speakers arrested, and chants criminalised. The message was clear. Sympathy for the Palestinian people, under occupation and siege, was too close to sympathy for Hamas. And that, in turn, was too close to terrorism.

This is Orwell's thoughtcrime made real. Not only must you not act violently, you must not think in ways that challenge the state's version of who is a terrorist and who is not.

In the United States, this logic has been used to equate criticism of Israel with antisemitism, a conflation that silences dissent while shielding state violence. Entire university departments have come under scrutiny. Student groups have been defunded. Academics have lost jobs. The suspicion is that they sympathise too much with the "wrong" side.

Yet this weaponisation of sympathy is not confined to the Middle East.

During the wars in Iraq and Afghanistan, journalists who reported sympathetically on civilian casualties were accused of undermining the troops or giving aid to the enemy. When whistleblower Chelsea Manning leaked evidence of U.S. military abuses, including the infamous *Collateral Murder* video showing a U.S. helicopter gunning down unarmed Iraqi civilians, the crime was not the killing. It was the revealing. Sympathy for Manning became, in itself, an act of political defiance.

The same logic appears in the treatment of whistleblowers like Edward Snowden or Julian Assange. Their work exposed mass surveillance, war crimes, and abuses of state power. But the response from many governments and media outlets was not to reckon with those crimes. It was to vilify the messengers and condemn those who defended them.

Sympathy, in these contexts, becomes subversion. It is seen not as a pathway to justice or reconciliation, but as a threat to national security. You are no longer innocent until proven guilty. You are suspect until proven loyal.

This marks a dangerous evolution in how terrorism is fought. It is no longer simply about preventing violence. It is about policing emotion, allegiance, and language. And it turns the war on terror into a war on humanity's most basic instincts, compassion, empathy, and the desire to understand.

When governments begin to monitor your sympathies, when laws are used to criminalise your sentiments, we are no longer in the realm of justice. We are in the realm of tyranny.

## Section 7: - Citizenship on Trial – When Your Passport Becomes a Threat

In today's security-obsessed world, citizenship is no longer a guarantee of protection. It can be revoked, downgraded, or reinterpreted based on suspicion, ancestry, or ideology. The passport you hold no longer says who you are. It says who the state allows you to be.

This weaponisation of citizenship has become a hallmark of modern counter-terrorism. Where once citizenship was an inviolable bond between individual and state, it is now conditional. You can be born in a country, live there all your life, pay taxes, raise children, and still find your status questioned, your rights suspended, and your very belonging challenged.

Take the UK's use of citizenship-stripping powers. Under the British Nationality Act, the Home Secretary has the power to revoke citizenship if it is deemed "conducive to the public good." What began as a rarely used power in the wake of 9/11 became routine by the mid-2010s. Dozens of Britons, often with dual heritage or links to Muslim-majority countries, had their citizenship removed, many while abroad, with no chance to appeal before it happened.

The most infamous case was that of Shamima Begum, the British teenager who travelled to Syria in 2015 to join ISIS. Stripped of her citizenship in 2019, Begum became a lightning rod for national debates on loyalty, extremism, and rehabilitation. While she had indeed made a grave choice, she was also a minor when radicalised, and left stateless by the decision. The Home Office insisted she could seek citizenship in Bangladesh, a country she had never visited and which refused to accept her. She was effectively exiled, not for actions proven in a court of law, but for associations and assumptions based on intelligence and headlines.

What was her real crime? Joining a terrorist group, or being a young Muslim woman who had made the wrong political choice?

In Australia, Canada, and France, similar powers have been introduced. In each case, the burden of proof is low, and the targets are disproportionately from immigrant or minority backgrounds. In the U.S., while the formal stripping of citizenship is rare, the logic persists. Muslim-Americans, particularly those born abroad, face heightened surveillance, repeated border searches, and a presumption of guilt in national security cases.

This is citizenship as a loyalty test.

The implications are profound. A second-tier system of rights is being created, one in which your race, religion, or politics can determine how 'safe' your citizenship is. It opens the door to a terrifying future, one where dissenting voices, protestors, or even journalists can be reclassified as enemies of the state, stripped of protection, and exiled, not for what they have done, but for what they believe.

And while these policies are sold as necessary tools in the fight against terror, they increasingly resemble the tactics of authoritarian regimes. China has long used internal passports to control movement. Russia and Israel have used citizenship status to disenfranchise critics and control populations. Now, liberal democracies are beginning to do the same under the guise of security.

What does it mean to be a citizen if your rights can be revoked at will? If your legal status is conditional on loyalty?

We are not just seeing the erosion of rights. We are seeing the erosion of belonging. A creeping redefinition of who is 'us' and who is 'them'. And in that redefinition, terrorism becomes not just an act but a label that justifies banishment.

The terrorist, in this model, is not someone who commits violence. It is someone who no longer deserves to belong.

## Section 8: - The Inversion – When Resistance Is the Crime, and Repression Is the Law

One of the most insidious transformations in modern counter-terrorism discourse is the inversion of moral logic, where resistance becomes the crime and repression becomes the law. It is a reversal that turns power into victimhood, protest into threat, and survival into subversion. It reframes the relationship between oppressor and oppressed, allowing the state to claim legitimacy even as it brutalises, while delegitimising the very people it harms.

This inversion is most clearly visible in occupied territories, where indigenous resistance to colonisation or military aggression is routinely framed as terrorism, while the occupier's violence is legalised, rationalised, and sanitised. Think of Gaza. When a stateless, blockaded people fight back with stones, with words, or even with crude rockets, they are labelled terrorists. But when a nuclear-armed state bombs homes, schools, and hospitals in the name of 'defence', it is considered an act of national security.

Such logic is not unique to Israel and Palestine. In the dying days of apartheid, Nelson Mandela and the African National Congress were officially designated as terrorists by the governments of the United States and the United Kingdom for daring to resist a system that legally segregated and oppressed an entire race. Rebellion was the crime. White minority rule was the law.

This same pattern holds across history. In colonial India, those who defied the British were imprisoned or executed as seditionists and terrorists. In Algeria, the French used torture and mass arrests to suppress independence movements. In Vietnam, U.S. forces treated resistance fighters as enemy combatants devoid of rights, while justifying widespread civilian killings under the umbrella of counter-insurgency.

In all of these cases, the label of 'terrorist' did not reflect the morality of the actions. It reflected the power to name.

As Noam Chomsky once noted: "Everyone's worried about stopping terrorism. Well, there's really an easy way: stop participating in it."

But in today's geopolitical landscape, that principle is rarely applied. Instead, resistance is criminalised, often through a pre-emptive logic that assumes anyone from a 'hostile' group is a latent terrorist. In Kashmir, in Xinjiang, and in parts of Africa and the Middle East, dissent is not simply discouraged. It is classified as terrorism from the outset.

Legal mechanisms reinforce this narrative. Anti-terror laws are often drafted so broadly that they criminalise speech, association, or support for resistance causes. In the U.S., providing "material support" to a designated terrorist group can mean sending a book, sharing a video, or fundraising for humanitarian aid. In France, Palestine solidarity groups have been banned under "glorification of terrorism" laws. In the UK, the Terrorism Act has been used to stop protestors under suspicion of ideology alone.

The inversion is near-total. Liberation movements are outlawed, while their oppressors are armed and funded.

Even global institutions often reinforce this narrative. The UN designates some groups as terrorists, yet remains paralysed in responding to state-sponsored mass violence. NATO intervenes against 'terror threats' in the Global South but offers no protection to civilians being bombed by its own allies.

Resistance, in this world, is only valid when it aligns with the strategic interests of the powerful. When Ukraine fights back against Russian aggression, it is heroic. When Palestinians resist occupation, they are terrorists. The difference is not in the method. It is in who holds the microphone.

And so, repression becomes the law, not by virtue of its morality, but by virtue of its legality. The state, with its courts, its weapons, and its PR machine, determines the narrative. Those who resist are cast not as victims of power, but as threats to order.

This is the world we have built, where the greatest crime is not violence, but defiance.

And in that world, terrorism is no longer about the nature of the act, but the identity of the actor.

## Section 9: - The Sympathiser Trap – When Solidarity Is Surveillance

In today's counter-terrorism paradigm, the danger is no longer limited to the so-called terrorist. It extends, by design, to those who speak out, show sympathy, or dare to question the narrative. This is the sympathiser trap, a chilling feature of modern surveillance states that criminalises not just action, but association, emotion, and even thought.

We've seen this play out time and again. Journalists, academics, human rights defenders, and ordinary citizens have been placed under watch, denied visas, raided, or prosecuted for supporting, or merely appearing to support, causes that challenge dominant geopolitical interests. The line between solidarity and suspicion is not just thin. It is deliberately blurred.

The United States' post-9/11 "War on Terror" expanded this trap exponentially. The Patriot Act introduced sweeping powers allowing the government to investigate anyone providing "material support" to designated terrorist organisations, a phrase so vague it has included humanitarian workers, lawyers, and even peace activists. In some cases, donations to legitimate NGOs operating in Gaza or Lebanon have been criminalised years later because the organisations were retroactively labelled as terrorist-affiliated.

In the UK, Palestine Action activists, including elderly nuns, priests, and even a 91-year-old woman, have been arrested under terrorism legislation for their non-violent protests against arms companies supplying weapons to Israel. Their crime was refusing to be silent and refusing to accept that justice for Palestinians is incompatible with British foreign policy.

In the U.S., Trump-era rhetoric cast entire movements such as Black Lives Matter, Antifa, and others as terrorist threats. "We are designating Antifa as a terrorist organisation," Trump tweeted in May 2020, with no legal basis to do so. By conflating dissent with terror, he fed the apparatus of surveillance and suspicion that already hovered over communities of colour, Muslims, and left-wing activists.

Meanwhile, pro-Israel advocacy groups have pushed to label the Boycott, Divestment, and Sanctions (BDS) movement as antisemitic or supportive of terrorism. U.S. states have passed legislation requiring employees or contractors to sign loyalty oaths disavowing BDS. In effect, you can lose your job or your public funding, not because you committed an act of violence, but because you chose to boycott a nation's policies.

This is not about stopping terrorism. It is about deterring solidarity.

And it stretches far beyond the West. In India, the Modi government has weaponised anti-terror laws to arrest students, poets, and activists critical of the state's treatment of Muslims. In Egypt, supporters of the Arab Spring were jailed en masse for "sympathising" with the banned Muslim Brotherhood. In Turkey, thousands have been detained under suspicion of supporting Kurdish insurgents, even if their only act was a Facebook post or attending a protest.

Once you broaden the definition of terrorism to include ideology, emotion, or cultural identity, then everyone is a suspect and solidarity becomes a crime.

It is worth recalling a powerful quote from Desmond Tutu, who warned:
"If you are neutral in situations of injustice, you have chosen the side of the oppressor."

But in today's world, choosing the side of the oppressed can get you labelled a threat to national security.

This weaponisation of surveillance does not stop with government. Big Tech algorithms, often trained on biased data, flag terms like "Free Palestine," "Allahu Akbar," or "resistance" as indicators of extremism. Entire online communities are shadow-banned, demonetised, or handed over to law enforcement, not because of any act of violence, but because they tell a different story.

And in this climate, self-censorship becomes survival. People learn to keep quiet, avoid certain terms, or delete posts from years past, not because they are guilty, but because innocence is no longer a defence. The mere appearance of sympathy can be enough to trigger surveillance, arrest, or ostracisation.

What this creates is not just a chilling effect. It is an ideological prison. It redefines citizenship as compliance and patriotism as silence. It teaches us that compassion must be measured, selective, and state-approved. That grief for the wrong victims is dangerous.

That rage at injustice must be muted if it falls on the wrong side of the geopolitical divide.

This is the sympathiser trap. And once set, it does not catch terrorists.

It catches truth-tellers.

# CONCLUSION TO PART III: -
# Protest, Resistance, and Rebellion

If Part I established that the word "terrorism" has no fixed definition, and Part II showed how states manipulate that ambiguity to justify their own violence, then Part III has revealed the tragic consequences for those who dare to resist. Whether in the streets of Minneapolis, the refugee camps of Gaza, or the courtrooms of London, we have seen how protest can be rebranded as extremism, how dissenters become suspects, and how entire communities are criminalised not for what they do, but for what they represent.

This is the dark inversion of justice in the modern era, where oppressors cloak themselves in legitimacy and those who resist are cast as terrorists. Language does not merely describe power; it creates it. And in a world where public perception can be more powerful than any court ruling, the label alone is enough to destroy lives, derail movements, and delegitimise entire causes.

Across Part III, we encountered the stories of those who resisted through marches, art, civil disobedience, and even armed struggle, and saw how quickly their actions could be reframed by those who control the narrative. We saw how guilt by association has replaced fair process, how nuns and students can be branded as terrorist sympathisers, and how the line between protest and prosecution is now razor thin. And we must ask, if no form of resistance is safe from the terrorism label, what resistance is left?

**Introduction to Part IV: The Global Consequences**

But the weaponisation of the word "terrorist" does not only affect individuals or movements. It corrodes the global order itself. Around the world, regimes cloak authoritarianism in the language of counterterrorism. Democracies justify sweeping surveillance, indefinite detention, and the erosion of civil liberties by invoking a perpetual war against an ill-defined enemy. The very foundations of international law and human rights are being shaken, not by bombs in markets, but by policies in parliaments.

In Part IV, we turn our gaze outward, beyond the protester and the prisoner, to the lawmakers and the lawbreakers. We examine how terrorism laws have become tools of repression, how international norms are selectively applied, and how the label of "terrorist" has been used to justify everything from drone assassinations to illegal invasions. We will ask whether the global war on terror has become a global licence for lawlessness and whether the world can reclaim its moral compass before the word "terrorism" becomes utterly meaningless.

# PART IV

# CHAPTER TWELVE

## Section 1: - The Legal Cage – How Terrorism Legislation Became a Toolkit for Authoritarian Control

In the aftermath of nearly every major terrorist attack in recent memory, the cry has been the same: "We must act to keep our people safe." The political response is often swift, symbolic, and severe. Laws are passed in a hurry, civil liberties quietly rolled back, and surveillance powers dramatically expanded. But what begins as a temporary emergency measure in the name of public safety has, over time, become a permanent framework of control.

From the USA PATRIOT Act after 9/11 to the UK's Prevent Strategy and Schedule 7 powers under the Terrorism Act 2000, the legislative legacy of terrorism has been the systematic erosion of rights once considered fundamental. These laws have granted governments extraordinary authority to detain without charge, to monitor private communications, to freeze assets, to criminalise association and speech, and to circumvent due process, all under the banner of "national security."

And the threshold for invoking these powers is remarkably low.

Consider Schedule 7 of the UK's Terrorism Act, which allows police and border officials to stop, search, and detain individuals without suspicion. Not on the basis of evidence. Not on the basis of intelligence. Just because they can. There is no requirement for "reasonable cause," no right to remain silent, and any refusal to answer questions may itself be treated as grounds for prosecution. As many lawyers and civil liberties campaigners have pointed out, this is not policing, it is profiling.

The law has become a pretext to harass journalists, intimidate activists, and silence dissenting voices. British journalist Glenn Greenwald, whose partner David Miranda was detained for nine hours under Schedule 7 in 2013, called it "a profound abuse of process." Miranda was never charged with any crime. His offence was simply being in possession of classified documents related to the Snowden leaks, documents that revealed the state's own breaches of international law.

What makes these powers especially dangerous is their elasticity. Governments argue that the definition of terrorism must be broad enough to include new and emerging threats. But that vagueness is precisely what allows it to be weaponised.

Protesting a military base? You may be investigated under terror laws. Organising a boycott of Israeli goods? Monitored as potential extremist activity. Taking part in a climate protest that disrupts traffic? In 2024, the UK government floated proposals to treat such actions as serious disruption under new counter-terror measures.

This is how authoritarianism works in the modern age, not through dramatic coups or jackbooted soldiers in the streets, but through the quiet expansion of executive power, legitimised by fear and ratified by law. Terrorism, once seen as an extraordinary threat, has become a convenient justification for a permanent state of exception.

The irony is bitter: laws passed to protect democracy are now the means by which democracy is hollowed out.

## Section 2: - The Surveillance State – Watching Everyone, Trusting No One

The war on terror has birthed something unprecedented in human history: a global surveillance state that peers into the lives of ordinary citizens with powers once reserved for the most totalitarian regimes. In the name of security, democratic governments have normalised spying on their own populations. The logic is seductive and dangerously simple: if terrorists can be anywhere, then everyone is a suspect. And if everyone is a suspect, then no one is truly free.

In the aftermath of 9/11, the United States led the charge. The PATRIOT Act gave sweeping authority to intelligence agencies to monitor phone calls, emails, bank transactions, and even library records. Soon, this model of governance by surveillance was exported globally. What began as a counterterrorism tool quickly morphed into a mechanism for political control. As Edward Snowden famously revealed in 2013, agencies like the NSA were not just watching suspected terrorists. They were watching everyone, allies and enemies, citizens and journalists, presidents and dissidents.

Britain followed suit with its own digital dragnet. The Investigatory Powers Act 2016, derided by critics as the "Snoopers' Charter," granted UK security services and police the right to store every citizen's browsing history for 12 months. It required telecommunications companies to cooperate in mass data retention and gave state agencies access to this data without meaningful judicial oversight. All in the name of counterterrorism. The line between legitimate investigation and blanket suspicion was erased.

What these laws share is not just scope but secrecy. They often operate in legal shadows, rubber-stamped by closed courts and shielded from democratic scrutiny. Worse, they expand and entrench themselves in times of crisis. The COVID-19 pandemic saw emergency surveillance measures deployed under the guise of public health. Facial recognition cameras were ramped up. Digital contact tracing became ubiquitous. The infrastructure of surveillance was now built into everyday life, not just as an extraordinary measure, but as a permanent feature.

The danger here is not just to privacy. It is to democracy itself. Surveillance chills dissent. It discourages activism. People are less likely to attend protests, speak freely, or associate with certain groups if they believe they are being watched. This is not theoretical. In the United States, Black Lives Matter activists were tracked and monitored. In the UK, Palestine Action protestors have been arrested and surveilled under terrorism frameworks. In France, environmental activists have faced criminal investigations usually reserved for organised crime or jihadist networks.

Once surveillance powers are in place, they are rarely rolled back. The political incentive to appear "tough on terror" outweighs concerns about civil liberties. Those who oppose these powers are branded naïve at best, or terrorist sympathisers at worst. As a result, most citizens quietly accept the trade-off: freedom for security, autonomy for the illusion of safety.

But what happens when the state misuses its surveillance powers? Or when they are turned inward, not against terrorists, but against teachers, journalists, climate protestors, or minority communities? This is not hypothetical. In India, surveillance technology has been used to monitor Muslim activists. In Israel, Pegasus spyware, developed by the NSO Group, was used not only to target criminals but also journalists and human rights defenders. In Hungary, Viktor Orbán's government used similar tools to watch political opponents and independent media.

And what of those who dare expose these abuses? Edward Snowden, arguably the most significant whistleblower of the 21st century, lives in exile in Russia after revealing the breadth of the NSA's global surveillance programme. He exposed how ordinary citizens were being monitored en masse by their governments under the pretext of national security. Far from being celebrated, Snowden became an international fugitive, cut off from his country, his family, and his freedom. His punishment sent a clear message: speak out, and you will be cast out.

And then there is Julian Assange.

In June 2024, after more than a decade of confinement, seven years inside the Ecuadorian embassy and five more in Britain's Belmarsh Prison, Assange was released as part of a plea deal. Extradited to a U.S. court in Saipan, he agreed to plead guilty to a single charge: conspiring to obtain and publish classified material. But as Assange himself explained to European lawmakers shortly after his release, he had in fact "pled guilty to journalism." Speaking before the Parliamentary Assembly of the Council of Europe in Strasbourg, Assange declared:

"I am not free today because the system worked. I am free today after years of incarceration because I pled guilty to journalism, to seeking information from a source, to informing the public what that information was. I did not plead guilty to anything else."

His case had always been about more than espionage or unauthorised leaks. At its core was the question of whether journalism that exposes war crimes, civilian deaths, and government lies can be tolerated in a system that brands truth-tellers as threats. Assange's WikiLeaks revelations, especially the "Collateral Murder" video and diplomatic cables exposing abuses in Iraq, Afghanistan, and beyond, pierced the veil of military and diplomatic secrecy.

By forcing Assange into a corner where freedom came at the cost of admission, the U.S. created a chilling precedent: that publishing uncomfortable truths about state power can be criminalised under the same logic used against actual terrorists. The physical damage to Assange was obvious, a man hollowed by isolation, deprived of health, family, and liberty. But the wider damage was more insidious: a warning to all future journalists, editors, whistleblowers, and truth-tellers. If they come for the publisher, no one is safe.

The irony is profound. In a world where "freedom" is the watchword of Western democracies, the tools of oppression, secrecy, surveillance, and silencing have become institutionalised. The line between democratic security and authoritarian control has blurred. And all it took was the invocation of that one magic word: terrorism.

## Section 3: - The Expanding Web – From Threats to Thoughts

The modern counter-terrorism landscape no longer hinges solely on the prevention of violence. It now operates in the nebulous territory of pre-crime, where intent, ideology, and even association can form the basis for state intervention. In this world, a thought expressed online, an unpopular opinion voiced in a classroom, or a political slogan shouted at a protest may be treated not just as a concern but as a potential act of terror in the making.

One of the most controversial examples of this phenomenon is the UK's Prevent programme, part of its broader CONTEST counter-terrorism strategy. Originally established to stop people from becoming terrorists or supporting terrorism, Prevent has evolved into a mechanism of pre-emptive suspicion, focused not on what someone has done, but what they might do in the future. Children as young as four have been referred for expressing "concerning" ideas. Teachers, doctors, and social workers are legally required to report signs of "radicalisation," a term that remains ill-defined and inconsistently applied.

For Muslim communities in particular, this has created a climate of fear and self-censorship. Reports from groups like Liberty and Amnesty International show that Prevent disproportionately targets Muslims, even in the absence of any concrete threat. Religious symbols, criticisms of British foreign policy, or simple expressions of solidarity with Palestine have all been flagged under the scheme. This is not terrorism prevention; it is thought policing.

The same logic has bled into policing more broadly. Consider the case of Palestine Action, a direct action group campaigning against UK complicity in Israeli war crimes by targeting weapons factories owned by Elbit Systems, Israel's largest arms manufacturer. Despite engaging in civil disobedience rather than violence, the group has been surveilled, raided, and prosecuted under terrorism laws. Some members face charges under the Serious Organised Crime and Police Act (SOCPA) and anti-terrorism legislation, even though their activities involve no threat to life.

Meanwhile, proscribed organisations such as the Ulster Defence Association (UDA), a loyalist paramilitary group responsible for dozens of murders and bombings during the Northern Ireland conflict, are allowed to march under police escort, without arrests or terrorism charges. When peaceful protestors are met with riot vans and violent paramilitary groups are met with accommodation, the law's uneven hand is laid bare. Who gets to be called a terrorist, it seems, is not about actions but allegiances.

Worse still, counter-terror measures are increasingly being used to suppress criticism of the state itself. In France, the government passed a law in 2021 aimed at fighting "Islamist separatism," which has been widely condemned as a vehicle for silencing Muslim dissent. In India, the Unlawful Activities Prevention Act (UAPA) has been used to arrest academics, journalists, and activists who criticise the Modi government's Hindu nationalist agenda. In the U.S., legislation once intended to prevent attacks on American soil is now used to monitor environmental activists and Black Lives Matter organisers.

This creep of counter-terrorism into political life reflects a dangerous shift in the state's priorities. Where terrorism was once understood as violence for political ends, it is now often understood as politics itself, especially when that politics challenges the status quo.

In a leaked UK Home Office memo from 2020, anti-capitalist and environmental movements were listed alongside white supremacist and Islamist threats under the rubric of "ideological extremism." The implication was clear: any organised attempt to challenge structural power, even peacefully, could fall within the scope of terrorism legislation. This is no longer about security. It is about control.

Even silence is no protection. In recent years, courts in various Western countries have handed down guilt by association verdicts. Being at a protest where graffiti was sprayed or a window was broken can lead to terrorism-related charges. Donating to a legal defence fund for an activist group under investigation can prompt police surveillance. Simply sharing articles deemed "radical" by authorities may be enough to land someone on a watchlist.

What emerges from all of this is a profound danger: the erosion of the boundary between dissent and terrorism. In the name of preventing violence, governments have embraced a logic that sees enemies everywhere. A child with a Palestinian flag becomes a subject of inquiry. A journalist reporting on a weapons shipment is branded a sympathiser. A lawyer defending a client accused of extremism is warned to watch their own associations.

The expanding web does not catch terrorists; it entangles the fabric of democracy itself. If mere ideas can be criminalised, then political discourse becomes a minefield. Free thought, the bedrock of any democratic society, is no longer free when it exists under surveillance.

And perhaps that is the point.

## Section 4: - Targeting Dissent – When Activism Becomes Extremism

The hallmark of a functioning democracy is the right to dissent, to challenge the status quo, to protest, to speak truth to power. But in the 21st-century security state, protest is increasingly seen not as a civic right but a national threat. The border between legitimate activism and "extremism" has been blurred, often deliberately, by governments keen to neutralise opposition and pacify unrest. The result is that movements for justice, equality, and environmental survival are now being met with surveillance, suppression, and the full force of counterterror laws.

In recent years, environmental campaigners, anti-racism protestors, and pro-Palestinian activists have all found themselves lumped in with groups labelled as "extremists." Police raids, pre-emptive arrests, electronic tagging, asset seizures, and even "terror-related" investigations have become increasingly common tactics. In the UK, members of Palestine Action, a non-violent direct-action group targeting Elbit Systems, an Israeli arms company with UK operations, have been arrested, prosecuted under terrorism-linked charges, and detained for long periods. Their crime? Throwing paint on weapons factories, blocking entrances, and exposing the role of British complicity in Israeli military operations.

The absurdity of the comparison is galling. A group of unarmed activists throwing red paint to symbolise Palestinian blood is framed as more dangerous than arms manufacturers shipping actual missiles into warzones. When protest targets business as usual, the law does not serve justice; it serves power.

The United States offers a similar picture. In 2020, the FBI classified so-called "eco-terrorism" as a top domestic terror threat, despite the complete absence of fatal incidents by such groups. Meanwhile, right-wing militias continued to grow in strength, organisation, and lethality. The Dakota Access Pipeline protests, led by Indigenous communities and climate activists at Standing Rock, were met with militarised police, rubber bullets, water cannons in freezing temperatures, and mass surveillance. Protestors were branded as agitators, infiltrated by private security firms, and charged with terrorism-related offences for acts of civil disobedience.

It is no coincidence that these repressive tactics align with the interests of oil companies, arms manufacturers, and security contractors. As writer Naomi Klein argued in *The Shock Doctrine*, crises are often used to justify the expansion of state and corporate power, and those who resist are branded as enemies of the state. Whether it is opposition to fracking in the UK, anti-coal protests in Germany, or climate blockades in Australia, the story is the same: activism is rebranded as extremism. Protest becomes peril.

Technology has only accelerated this trend. In France, Germany, and the US, facial recognition is now being used to track protestors before, during, and after demonstrations. In India, surveillance drones and internet shutdowns are deployed to control and suppress dissent in regions like Kashmir. In Israel and Palestine, military-grade surveillance software such as Pegasus has been turned inward, not just on "enemies" but on civil society, journalists, and lawyers.

Meanwhile, Western leaders still posture as defenders of liberty. They quote Voltaire and Martin Luther King while their governments detain climate scientists and drag young people through the courts for gluing themselves to roads. The contradiction is staggering. The same states that trumpet democracy as a core value are the ones criminalising those who dare to demand it be lived, not just claimed.

Even satire and art are not immune. In Turkey, artists and cartoonists have been jailed for mocking President Erdoğan. In Egypt, rap lyrics and TikTok videos have led to terrorism charges. In Hungary, academic institutions have been gutted for studying gender or migration. In Israel, human rights NGOs that expose state abuses are labelled as "terror supporters" and denied funding or legal standing.

In all these cases, the word "terrorism" hovers just beneath the surface. It does not need to be spoken directly; the mere suggestion that a group might be radical, or "linked" to radicals, is enough. Funding dries up, the media turns hostile, and the state moves in. The chilling effect on civic life is immense.

So the question must be asked: if you strip away the right to protest, if you surveil every gathering, if you criminalise organising, what kind of society remains?

The answer is not a free one. It is a society where silence is safety, where justice is subversive, where opposition is treated as sabotage.

In such a world, the line between activist and terrorist is no longer legal or moral. It is political. It is drawn by those in power to serve power.

## Section 5: - The Chilling Effect on Civil Liberties

Across liberal democracies, once-vital spaces of dissent are slowly being extinguished under the expanding shadow of terrorism legislation. Laws originally designed to target violent extremists have morphed into sprawling frameworks that now reach deep into the realm of non-violent protest, journalism, academic research, and even online expression. The result is a chilling effect, a widespread fear among individuals, activists, and organisations that their actions, words, or associations could be reinterpreted as criminal under vague and politically malleable definitions of terrorism.

In the United Kingdom, the evolution of this phenomenon is particularly instructive. After the introduction of the Terrorism Act 2000, the state was granted broad powers to designate organisations as "proscribed," effectively criminalising not only the group itself, but any form of material or symbolic support. While this law was ostensibly aimed at violent groups, it has increasingly been applied to peaceful political activism, especially those challenging state interests or foreign allies such as Israel. The 2023 arrest of Palestine Action protestors, many of whom were engaged in non-violent civil disobedience against Elbit Systems, an Israeli arms manufacturer with UK sites, was a watershed moment. Among those detained were elderly nuns, Christian clergy, and even a 91-year-old woman who had merely protested outside a factory gate. All were arrested under anti-terror laws.

Contrast this with the PSNI's prior role in "escorting" marches by the Ulster Defence Association (UDA), a proscribed paramilitary organisation responsible for dozens of murders during the Troubles. No arrests were made for simply participating in or organising these UDA-aligned events. The contrast is damning. One group, responsible for lethal violence, was handled with deference. Another, whose crimes were spray-painting buildings and blockading gates, was treated as a national security threat. What this signals is not the equal application of law, but the selective enforcement of ideology.

The danger here is not only the erosion of civil liberties, but the normalisation of fear as a political tool. Journalists who investigate counter-terror practices risk being accused of aiding terrorism. Academics researching conflict zones may fall foul of "material support" statutes. Protestors who align themselves with the victims of state violence, particularly when that state is a Western ally, may find themselves labelled not as peace advocates but as sympathisers to terror.

This climate of suspicion and surveillance also disproportionately affects Muslim communities. As the UN Special Rapporteur on Counterterrorism and Human Rights has repeatedly noted, broad counter-terror frameworks have led to discriminatory profiling, raids without warrants, and a policing culture that prioritises intelligence-gathering over community engagement. Mosques are monitored. Charities are blacklisted. Youth organisations are infiltrated. The message is clear: your rights are conditional, your freedoms suspended, and your loyalties forever under suspicion.

In the United States, the FBI's Countering Violent Extremism (CVE) programme raised similar alarm. Framed as a preventative initiative, it relied on unproven behavioural indicators to identify potential radicals, resulting in the surveillance of Muslim students, schoolchildren, and community members based on nothing more than political views or cultural background. Civil liberties groups such as the ACLU denounced it as a form of pre-crime policing, where thought and association, rather than actions, trigger suspicion.

In this environment, dissent becomes dangerous. Solidarity becomes subversive. And the very essence of democratic participation, freedom of speech, protest, and association, is sacrificed at the altar of security. As Professor David Lyon put it in his analysis of the surveillance state, "The panoptic gaze no longer watches the guilty, but the potentially disloyal."

What is most disturbing is that this is not the result of a coup, a revolution, or a military takeover. It is the result of legislation passed in parliaments, executed by bureaucrats, justified by ministers, and too often ignored by the public. It is a slow, quiet, bureaucratic creep towards authoritarianism, one bill, one arrest, one headline at a time.

## Section 6: - The Israel Effect – Redefining Terrorism by Proxy

To understand the current trajectory of global terror laws, one must examine the extent to which the definition of "terrorism" has become distorted, not through consensus, but through influence. Chief among those shaping this redefinition is the State of Israel, whose long-standing battle against Palestinian resistance has not only informed its own domestic policies but has increasingly set the tone for how other Western democracies define, identify, and respond to dissent. What we are witnessing is the export of a legal and rhetorical framework in which Israel's strategic interests are fused with the West's definition of terrorism.

Since 2001, Israel has succeeded in having most Palestinian armed groups labelled as terrorist organisations across the Western world. But the designation has not stopped there. Groups such as the Boycott, Divestment and Sanctions (BDS) movement, Palestine Action, and even humanitarian NGOs have found themselves smeared as being either "terror-adjacent" or "enablers of extremist ideology." In some cases, simply criticising Israel's actions is construed as veiled support for terrorism.

This did not happen in a vacuum. It reflects a deep and strategic alignment between Israel and major Western powers, especially the United States and the United Kingdom, whereby terrorism is not defined by methods, but by the target. Violence or resistance against Israel, regardless of scale or context, is terrorism. Conversely, military campaigns conducted by Israel, even those resulting in tens of thousands of civilian deaths, are labelled self-defence.

This logic has bled into domestic policy across the West. Laws initially passed to combat Al-Qaeda or ISIS have been quietly repurposed to surveil, restrict, and prosecute those who criticise Israeli policy or support Palestinian rights. The Prevent Strategy in the UK and anti-BDS laws in over 30 US states are clear examples of this shift. In France, pro-Palestinian protests have been banned under public order laws and "support for terror" allegations. In Germany, even Holocaust survivors critical of Israel have been silenced under accusations of antisemitism and radicalisation.

A pivotal moment came in 2024, when a cross-party coalition of MPs in the UK voted in favour of expanding the definition of terrorism to include "psychological harm" and "ideological incitement," terms so vague they could apply to anything from protest slogans to academic lectures. This followed sustained lobbying from pro-Israel groups, citing the rise in anti-Israel activism after the 2023 Gaza assault. The legislative note accompanying the bill made multiple references to "online radicalisation" and "emotional harm to communities," a dog-whistle aimed squarely at silencing criticism of Israel under the guise of national security.

The effect is not just legislative, it is cultural. The label of "terrorism" has become less about violence and more about narrative control. In this ecosystem, Israel is not merely a state defending itself, it is a model for how modern democracies can manipulate fear, blur legal lines, and redefine threat in a way that serves state interests while delegitimising opposition.

The consequence is catastrophic. By allowing one country's highly contested political narrative to shape the legal frameworks of multiple others, the West has undermined its own commitment to objectivity, fairness, and human rights. Dissent is recast as danger. Resistance is criminalised. And the public, increasingly disoriented by the moral inversion, either disengages or conforms.

As Professor Richard Falk, former UN Special Rapporteur on Human Rights in the Occupied Territories, warned:

*"What Israel has succeeded in doing is exporting a form of legal exceptionalism. In its case, the law doesn't apply. In the rest of the world, the law is rewritten in its image."*

This is the Israel Effect. And if left unchecked, it will transform anti-terror laws from instruments of safety into weapons of ideological repression, not only silencing Palestinian solidarity but hollowing out the very freedoms that define open societies.

## Section 7: - The Dangerous Precedent

When democracies adopt vague, elastic definitions of terrorism, they do not merely increase the number of people who can be accused—they degrade the meaning of the term itself. What began as a label meant to describe acts of violence against civilians for political ends has now become an ideological dragnet, capable of ensnaring protestors, journalists, whistleblowers, and even humanitarian workers. The result is not greater security. It is greater obedience.

The precedent being set is simple but devastating. If a state can determine what constitutes terrorism based not on what is done, but who it is done to or who is doing it, then any dissent can be treated as a threat. A flag waved in solidarity, a chant at a march, a critical article—these can all be interpreted as "extremist activity" if the state chooses to define them that way.

And many now are.

We have seen British police use counter-terror powers to investigate peaceful protestors. In the U.S., journalists critical of Israeli policy have found themselves on government watchlists. In Germany and France, pro-Palestinian speech has been banned or criminalised under anti-terrorism and hate speech laws, even when there is no incitement or violence involved.

The precedent is especially troubling because it is infectious. Once one country widens the definition of terrorism to criminalise unpopular opinion, others follow. Laws passed in the aftermath of the 9/11 attacks were justified by necessity. Now, similar laws are justified by imitation. Legislators point to "global best practice," citing what others have done as cover for what they are doing.

Consider the following examples:

- Australia's 2023 "Ideological Threats" Amendment Bill proposed adding vague references to "belief-based extremism," with no requirement of violence or planned violence, in part inspired by rising support for Palestinian rights.

- Canada's 2024 Security and Community Resilience Act introduced criminal penalties for "public justification of terror," which human rights groups warned could include merely expressing understanding for why a resistance group forms in an occupied territory.

- In Ireland, proposed legal changes would allow evidence obtained under surveillance alone, without charge, to be used in preventing public gatherings deemed "ideologically sensitive."

These laws, intentionally or not, signal that motive no longer matters. Even if an act is non-violent, even if it is constitutionally protected, even if it is morally grounded—if it challenges the wrong interests, it can be deemed terrorism.

This is the true danger of the precedent. It is not only illiberal—it is self-replicating. Once the rule of law becomes the rule of interpretation, all rights become privileges, subject to withdrawal without notice.

More worrying still is that the public has shown a high tolerance for this erosion. In an age of fear, uncertainty, and hyper-partisan media, people are easily persuaded to trade rights for reassurance. They are told the laws are not meant for them, but for the "radicals." Yet history is littered with examples of democracies turning their toughest laws inward.

Terrorism, once a term of moral horror, is now becoming a tool of political convenience. If today's protestor can be tomorrow's terrorist, then freedom itself becomes conditional. That is not a theory—it is happening.

As former UN Secretary-General Kofi Annan once said:

*"The biggest danger in fighting terror is becoming what you oppose."*

That is the precipice we now stand on. The label that once united the world against atrocity is being reshaped into a weapon of institutionalised paranoia, aimed at the very people democracy is meant to protect.

## Section 8: - From Law to Loyalty – The Rise of Compelled Conformity

In this new age of counter-terrorism creep, legality is no longer enough. The question is not just what you do, but what you believe. Increasingly, citizens are being coerced not simply to obey the law, but to demonstrate allegiance to the state, to its allies, and to its version of events. Neutrality is no longer tolerated. Silence is suspect. And dissent is dangerous.

Nowhere is this more evident than in the demand that individuals and institutions publicly denounce terrorism, but only certain kinds. Protesters must issue disclaimers. Teachers are required to spot "radicalisation" in their students. Charities must vet every partner and publication. All of it feeds a growing system of compelled conformity, where your political survival depends on your willingness to echo the state's talking points.

It is a subtle but seismic shift, from laws that prohibit harmful acts to a culture that punishes unsanctioned beliefs.

The UK's *Prevent* strategy, part of its broader counter-terrorism policy, has come under repeated criticism for targeting Muslim communities disproportionately. Schoolchildren have been reported to police for drawing pictures of mosques. University lecturers have been asked to monitor students' political opinions. The underlying assumption is clear: certain communities must constantly prove they are not a threat.

But compelled loyalty extends beyond the Muslim world. In the wake of Israel's war on Gaza, employees in Western universities, cultural institutions, and media outlets have been sacked or suspended for expressing support for Palestinian rights, even when expressed peacefully, legally, and compassionately. In the US, the CEO of a law firm publicly rescinded job offers to students at Ivy League universities after they signed statements condemning Israel's actions. Solidarity was equated with extremism, moral conscience with ideological deviance.

This tactic of demanding declarations of loyalty has long been associated with authoritarian regimes. In Stalin's USSR, Mao's China, or Pinochet's Chile, it was not enough to be obedient; one had to be affirmatively obedient. In the words of George Orwell:

*"Orthodoxy is not thinking—not needing to think. Orthodoxy is unconsciousness."*

That same orthodoxy is now being embedded in the policies of democratic states. Even humanitarian organisations are under pressure. NGOs offering aid in Gaza, for instance, have faced defunding simply for refusing to condemn Hamas with sufficient vigour, even though their stated missions are neutral and lifesaving.

Meanwhile, those who call for ceasefires or diplomacy find themselves labelled "terror sympathisers." Their crime is failing to conform to the dominant narrative.

And so a hierarchy of acceptable empathy emerges. Ukrainian civilians deserve support; Gazan civilians raise suspicion. Jewish trauma must be remembered; Palestinian trauma must be rationalised. One people's grief inspires solidarity, the other's silence. This is not the architecture of liberal democracy; it is the scaffolding of thought control.

Where counterterrorism once focused on preventing violence, it is now drifting toward policing alignment. Citizens are being trained, gently at first, to police each other. Employers monitor employees. Social media users mass-report dissent. The surveillance state is no longer just external; it is internalised.

What we are witnessing is not just a war on terrorism; it is the weaponisation of agreement.

When conformity is a condition of employment and neutrality is proof of disloyalty, freedom becomes little more than a slogan. The greatest irony is this: in the name of fighting terror, we are building systems that mirror the very regimes we once condemned.

In this world, democracy does not die with bombs. It dies when loyalty replaces liberty, and when silence is no longer safe.

# CHAPTER THIRTEEN

## Section 1: - The Collapse of Moral Authority

In the early years of the 21st century, the idea of a rules-based international order was often invoked as a moral compass, an architecture supposedly rooted in universal principles: sovereignty, human rights, justice, and restraint. Yet by 2025, that compass appears not merely broken but discarded. The very nations that claimed to uphold this order have, time and again, acted outside it, justifying unilateral military action, supporting regimes that commit atrocities, and selectively applying laws based on geopolitical interest rather than universal standards.

International law, once a post-war project aimed at protecting civilians and restraining power, has become increasingly irrelevant in a world where the powerful rewrite the rules on the fly. The clearest evidence of this erosion is found in the growing normalisation of extrajudicial killings, drone assassinations, illegal occupations, and collective punishments, all carried out with impunity by states that dismiss criticism as naïve or disloyal.

Perhaps the most striking example lies in the way military interventions are framed. In 2003, the United States and its allies invaded Iraq under the pretext of weapons of mass destruction, an allegation proven false yet never leading to prosecution or accountability. Millions were displaced or killed, a nation destabilised, and a new generation of terrorists born from the ruins. No international tribunal was convened. No leaders were charged. And no reparations were paid. Compare that to the swift condemnations and sanctions levied against weaker states or rebel groups for far less destructive actions.

This disparity is not lost on the Global South, where cynicism toward Western declarations of "liberty" and "human rights" has grown. As Western states ignore international norms when inconvenient, others feel emboldened to do the same, undermining any notion of a shared legal or moral framework. If international law is only enforced against the powerless, then it is not law at all but a weapon of politics.

Worse still, this lawlessness is being rebranded as virtue. The United States justifies drone strikes deep into sovereign territories as "self-defence." Israel calls its occupation of Palestinian land "security." Russia frames its invasion of Ukraine as "liberation." China jails Uyghur Muslims in "re-education" camps to promote "stability." Language has become a tool not of truth but of absolution, where any horror can be renamed until it sounds like protection.

## Section 2: - Vigilant States – When Governments Go Rogue

There was a time when vigilantism was the mark of disorder, an indication that the state had failed to uphold law and order, prompting individuals or groups to take justice into their own hands. But what happens when the state itself becomes the vigilante? When it decides who lives or dies without oversight, invades without permission, or punishes without due process? Increasingly, that is the reality in global politics: governments acting as judge, jury, and executioner on the world stage.

From Washington to Riyadh, from Tel Aviv to Moscow, powerful states are operating as self-authorised enforcers, deploying military and economic power beyond their borders without international approval. In doing so, they no longer even pretend to seek permission from global institutions like the United Nations. They offer rationales, such as "pre-emptive defence," "war on terror," or "national interest," that paper over what is essentially global vigilantism.

Consider the United States drone strike in January 2020 that killed Iranian General Qassem Soleimani in Baghdad. It was carried out on the territory of a third-party state, Iraq, against a foreign official, without a formal declaration of war. The United States justified it as self-defence. But by any legal standard, it was an act of assassination. There was no trial. No evidence presented. No tribunal convened. Only a missile strike and a statement from the President. This is the new model of justice: fast, remote, and irreversible.

Israel's own policies have followed a similar pattern. Long accused of operating beyond the boundaries of international law, it has executed cross-border strikes, assassinated political opponents, and bombed civilian infrastructure, all under the broad banner of "self-defence." In 2025, the pre-emptive strikes against Iran and Qatar were conducted with no oversight, no warning, and no consequences. The world, for the most part, shrugged.

This shift has been enabled by a complicit media and weakened multilateral institutions. The United Nations, frequently paralysed by the veto powers of its most powerful members, has become largely symbolic in the face of aggression by those very powers. Meanwhile, human rights bodies are dismissed as partisan, while investigative journalists are branded as enemies, some jailed, some exiled, some killed.

When states become vigilantes, the rule of law becomes the rule of the strong. The message is clear: if you have enough power, you do not need legitimacy. You can act unilaterally, violate sovereignty, and discard international norms, all without fear of prosecution or retribution.

This is not just a legal crisis. It is a moral one. Because once the idea takes root that some nations are above the law, others will stop respecting it altogether. That is the beginning of global disorder, not one rooted in chaos, but in calculated, institutional lawlessness disguised as defence.

## Section 3: - The Death of Accountability

In a world where states act as enforcers and institutions buckle under pressure, the final casualty is accountability. Once a cornerstone of democratic governance and international order, it is now little more than a slogan, invoked in press briefings and ignored in practice.

This collapse did not happen overnight. It is the result of decades of erosion: laws bent to suit expediency, war crimes rebranded as national security, and public inquiries neutered by political influence. The mechanisms designed to hold power in check—courts, tribunals, watchdogs, journalism—are under sustained attack or simply bypassed. As the global war on terror expanded in scope, so too did the excuses for state violence, carried out with impunity and often celebrated at home.

Take the International Criminal Court (ICC). Set up to prosecute the worst crimes—genocide, war crimes, crimes against humanity—it was once hailed as a leap forward for justice. But in practice, the ICC has been used disproportionately against African leaders, while powerful Western or allied nations remain untouchable. When the court dared to investigate potential United States or Israeli war crimes, both countries refused to recognise its authority. In fact, the United States threatened sanctions against ICC judges. So much for justice.

Then there is the United Nations Security Council, a body ostensibly responsible for maintaining international peace. But with five permanent members wielding veto power, it has become paralysed on key issues. Russia can invade Ukraine with impunity; the United States can veto any resolution condemning Israeli military actions. There is no accountability, only geopolitics dressed up as diplomacy.

The case of Israel is perhaps the most glaring. With widespread documentation of potential war crimes in Gaza, from targeting ambulances and journalists to using starvation as a weapon, Israel has still faced no meaningful consequences. The reason? It has powerful allies, chief among them the United States. As long as those alliances remain intact, accountability remains a distant dream.

Even public scrutiny has been dulled. Whistleblowers like Edward Snowden and Julian Assange revealed grave abuses of power, including mass surveillance, war crimes, and diplomatic cover-ups. But rather than being honoured, they were hunted. Assange spent fourteen years in detention. Snowden lives in exile. The message is clear: do not reveal the truth if it embarrasses the powerful.

In the absence of justice, states have resorted to performative accountability, including internal reviews, redacted reports, and delayed inquiries. These mechanisms give the appearance of oversight while delivering none. They are not designed to uncover the truth but to control the narrative.

As accountability dies, cynicism grows. Citizens lose faith in international law, human rights treaties, and the idea that justice applies to all. This erosion does not just empower dictators; it corrodes democracies from within. Because if a democratic state can kill, silence, or spy without consequence, how different is it from the regimes it once condemned?

The death of accountability is not an abstract crisis. It is the quiet, ongoing dismantling of the very principles that underpin a just and peaceful world. Without it, the powerful will continue to act with impunity, and the powerless will continue to pay the price.

## Section 4: - Humanitarian Law in Freefall

International humanitarian law, the laws of war, was created not to prevent all conflict but to place limits on it. Rooted in the Geneva Conventions and shaped by centuries of custom, it seeks to distinguish between combatants and civilians, to prohibit torture, and to limit suffering. In the modern era of asymmetrical warfare, counter-terrorism operations, and digital surveillance, these laws are being stretched to breaking point, ignored when inconvenient, weaponised when useful, and rewritten by those who wage war with impunity.

The rules of engagement that once defined the battlefield are now rendered moot by drone strikes in sovereign nations, cyber warfare without attribution, and economic blockades that starve civilian populations. The concept of proportionality, a bedrock of humanitarian law, has become meaningless in an era where military responses to low-level threats include flattening entire city blocks. Collateral damage is no longer an unfortunate consequence of war; it is the war.

Nowhere is this more evident than in Gaza, Yemen, or Afghanistan. Civilian infrastructure, including hospitals, schools, and refugee camps, has been repeatedly targeted or destroyed under the pretext of eliminating terrorists. Military forces claim compliance with international law even as images of bombed-out maternity wards flood our screens. Legal language is twisted to justify the unjustifiable. The laws have not failed; they have been deliberately bypassed.

Humanitarian law requires the protection of civilians, yet the very definition of a "combatant" has become dangerously elastic. In occupied territories or conflict zones, any male over a certain age is routinely deemed a legitimate target. Individuals labelled as "sympathisers," "accomplices," or even "future threats" can be summarily executed without charge or trial. These extrajudicial killings are often justified through secret legal opinions and intelligence reports that are never made public.

When violations are exposed, the legal system either stalls or shifts the blame. Investigations into alleged war crimes are frequently led by the very institutions accused of them. Military inquiries clear their own personnel. National courts refuse jurisdiction. International courts are rendered impotent by lack of access, political pressure, or veto powers. The result is a kind of legal nihilism, a world in which law exists but is not enforced.

Even language has been corrupted. Terms such as "human shields," "surgical strikes," and "defensive operations" are euphemisms that sanitise mass death. Civilian casualties are described as "regrettable but necessary." Starvation is "economic pressure." Siege is "containment." The law is not only violated; it is linguistically laundered.

Technological warfare has only accelerated this erosion. Drones allow countries to kill at a distance, reducing human life to pixels on a screen. Autonomous weapons and AI targeting systems introduce layers of abstraction, where accountability is not only avoided but automated. Who is responsible when a drone strike kills a wedding party: the operator, the programmer, or the commander who gave the order?

Meanwhile, the public, bombarded by conflicting narratives, becomes numb. If every act of violence can be legally rationalised, then none of it feels illegal. If every side claims compliance with humanitarian law, then the very idea of a moral war becomes absurd. In this chaos, the law is no longer a shield for the vulnerable; it is a tool for the powerful.

International humanitarian law is not just in crisis; it is in freefall. Unless states recommit to its principles, empower neutral bodies to enforce it, and hold violators accountable regardless of their alliances or influence, it risks becoming a relic, a noble ideal buried beneath the rubble of modern warfare.

## Section 5: - When the Watchdogs Fall Silent

In theory, a robust network of international organisations, human rights groups, and legal institutions exists to monitor state behaviour, expose abuses, and demand accountability. In practice, many of these watchdogs have been muzzled, ignored, co-opted, or overwhelmed. When the institutions meant to uphold justice begin to look away, or worse, lend legitimacy to injustice, the global system begins to rot from the inside.

The United Nations, once seen as a moral compass and guardian of peace, is increasingly paralysed by geopolitical gridlock. The Security Council, hamstrung by the veto powers of permanent members, has become a theatre of power rather than a tool of peace. When gross human rights abuses occur, from the invasion of Ukraine to the bombardment of Gaza, resolutions are drafted only to be struck down by allied vetoes. Justice is traded for diplomacy. Civilians pay the price.

Even within the UN's own bodies, inconsistencies abound. The Human Rights Council, long criticised for allowing authoritarian regimes to sit in judgement of others, often issues contradictory or toothless condemnations. Meanwhile, special rapporteurs, independent experts charged with reporting on abuses, face political pressure, harassment, or defunding when their findings threaten powerful interests. Their reports gather dust while the bombs fall.

Outside the UN system, international courts are no better. The International Criminal Court (ICC), for all its symbolic weight, has struggled to enforce its rulings. Its warrants, such as the one issued in 2023 for Russian President Vladimir Putin, are often unenforceable against leaders of powerful nations. In contrast, leaders of smaller or weaker states, particularly in Africa or the

Middle East, are swiftly prosecuted. Justice, it seems, is not blind; it sees wealth and power all too clearly.

In recent years, the erosion of trust in institutions has extended to NGOs and civil society groups. Once respected voices like Amnesty International and Human Rights Watch have found themselves caught in a web of political attacks, accused of bias or delegitimising states. Their access is blocked, their funding threatened, and their legitimacy undermined, not because they are wrong, but because they are inconvenient.

Media, too, plays a role in the muting of watchdogs. Investigative journalism has been gutted by budget cuts, ownership consolidation, and government hostility. Whistleblowers like Julian Assange and Edward Snowden, who exposed grave state abuses, are criminalised while those who committed the abuses go unpunished. When those who expose wrongdoing are labelled enemies of the state, a chilling message is sent: silence is safer than truth.

Even democratic nations have become complicit. Western governments that once funded or supported international oversight mechanisms now do so selectively, championing them when enemies are in the dock and ignoring them when allies stand accused. The United Kingdom, for example, has increasingly questioned the legitimacy of international legal rulings that do not favour its interests. The United States has refused to ratify the Rome Statute, shielding its military from ICC jurisdiction. Hypocrisy has replaced principle.

This crisis of watchdog institutions is not just a legal or diplomatic failure; it is a moral one. When justice becomes optional, when oversight is negotiable, and when power determines accountability, the very foundation of a rules-based international order begins to crumble. If there is one lesson history teaches with brutal clarity, it is this: silence in the face of injustice is not neutrality; it is complicity.

The watchdogs, once guardians of conscience, are now struggling to be heard. Some have been silenced by force. Others by fatigue. Others still by the slow realisation that in a world dominated by powerful actors with no intention of playing by the rules, barking can seem futile.

But the truth remains: their silence allows the worst to thrive.

## Section 6: - Selective Memory and Western Exceptionalism

Western democracies have long styled themselves as defenders of liberty, guardians of human rights, and champions of international law. But history, when remembered in full, tells a different story. Selective memory is the lifeblood of exceptionalism, and nowhere is this more evident than in the West's approach to terrorism, war, and justice.

Consider the glorification of past wars. In the United Kingdom, annual remembrance ceremonies pay homage to soldiers killed in the World Wars, yet rarely acknowledge the millions of colonial subjects who died fighting in Britain's name, or those who were killed resisting its rule. In the United States, the 9/11 attacks are commemorated with solemn gravity, but the millions who perished in the "War on Terror" that followed are rendered invisible. Iraq, Afghanistan, Libya—countries devastated by Western interventions—are footnotes in the narrative of American heroism.

This forgetfulness is not accidental; it is a form of political engineering. Western societies are taught to see their own violence as noble, their interventions as necessary, and their surveillance as responsible. When abuses occur, they are "mistakes" or "isolated incidents." When others commit the same acts, they are labelled as terrorism, atrocities, or war crimes.

The doctrine of exceptionalism permits not only moral evasion but legal impunity. The United States, for instance, has never been held to account for the use of torture at Abu Ghraib or Guantánamo Bay. The architects of those policies walk free, write memoirs, and appear on television as respected commentators. Meanwhile, whistleblowers like Chelsea Manning and Edward Snowden are exiled, punished, or smeared for daring to expose the truth.

Western exceptionalism also permeates the media. News coverage of terrorism starkly contrasts depending on the perpetrator. A white gunman in the United States is often described as "mentally ill" or "a lone wolf." A Muslim attacker is almost immediately branded a "terrorist," regardless of motive or mental state. Palestinian resistance is terrorism; Israeli airstrikes are "precision defence." The same act is judged not by its nature, but by the actor's identity.

This hypocrisy extends to international diplomacy. Western leaders routinely invoke human rights to criticise adversaries like China, Russia, or Iran, yet ignore or defend allies who commit equal or worse abuses. Saudi Arabia, for instance, continues to receive arms and diplomatic cover despite its brutal war in Yemen and the murder of journalist Jamal Khashoggi. Israel is afforded unflinching support even as its actions in Gaza draw comparisons to ethnic cleansing and collective punishment.

This is not just double standards; it is a moral collapse dressed as strategic interest.

Selective memory also means ignoring the long shadow of colonialism. The borders drawn by British and French empires, the coups supported by American intelligence agencies, and the resource plunder that financed European wealth are not ancient history. They are the roots of modern instability, from the Sahel to South Asia. Yet Western states rarely acknowledge their role in sowing the seeds of radicalisation, displacement, and violence. Instead, they focus only on the symptoms, never the disease.

In academic and political discourse, this exceptionalism has been dressed up in intellectual respectability. Concepts like "civilisational values" or "Western democratic norms" are used to imply superiority. The idea that "our way of life" must be protected, by force if necessary, has justified surveillance, war, and repression. But as the cracks in Western societies widen, from racial injustice to democratic decay, the myth of superiority rings increasingly hollow.

As long as the West clings to the idea that it stands above the fray, that its violence is defensive, its power benevolent, and its past irrelevant, it will fail to reckon with the very forces it claims to oppose. Terrorism will be misunderstood. Resistance will be mislabelled. Justice will remain an illusion for those who suffer at the sharp end of power.

There is no path to global justice that does not begin with self-reflection. And there is no redemption for democracies that remember only the glory and forget the guilt.

## Section 7: - Israel's Influence on the Language of Terror

If one state has played a disproportionate role in shaping the modern definition of terrorism, it is Israel. Not only through its policies, but through its ability to influence how acts of violence, resistance, and dissent are labelled globally. Over the decades, Israel has positioned itself as the eternal victim of terror, a framing that grants it immense political capital and moral leeway in defining who is a terrorist and what constitutes terrorism.

This influence is not limited to rhetoric. It permeates legislation, diplomacy, and media narratives. From the moment Palestinian resistance began to take organised forms, whether through armed struggle or political protest, it was swiftly categorised as terrorism. The context of occupation, dispossession, and apartheid was erased.

The cause, no matter how rooted in international law or human rights, was silenced under a single, unchallengeable label: terrorist.

Once that label sticks, the consequences are devastating. It justifies disproportionate retaliation. It silences diplomatic criticism. It removes the need for negotiation. It turns a political conflict into a security issue, one where only one side is recognised as having the right to defend itself.

Israeli leaders have been unapologetic in their use of this framing. Prime Minister Benjamin Netanyahu, a key architect of Israel's global security doctrine, has repeatedly denied that Palestinians have any right to resist. In 2014, during Israel's assault on Gaza, Netanyahu declared: "Israel uses missile defence to protect its civilians. Hamas uses civilians to protect its missiles." The statement, while rhetorically effective, flipped reality. It cast Israel as the sole victim and any Palestinian casualty as self-inflicted or the product of 'human shields.'

In a 2021 interview, when asked if Palestinians had a right to self-defence, Netanyahu curtly responded: "No. Because they are the aggressor." This denial of even the theoretical legitimacy of Palestinian resistance, peaceful or otherwise, has been repeated across Israeli political circles and accepted, often without question, by many in the West.

The Israeli government's framing has deeply influenced Western anti-terror laws. Definitions of terrorism in the UK's Terrorism Act 2000, the US Patriot Act, and the EU's Framework Decision on Combating Terrorism all contain language that conveniently mirrors Israeli terminology. Terms like "public intimidation," "serious disruption," or "political aims by violent means" are elastic enough to criminalise civil disobedience, particularly when it targets allies like Israel.

This influence extends to domestic policing. Peaceful protest movements critical of Israel, such as Palestine Action in the UK, have been surveilled, raided, and arrested under terrorism-related powers. Meanwhile, far-right Israeli nationalist marches, even when led by groups with histories of incitement and violence, receive police protection and are rarely scrutinised as security threats.

This asymmetry reveals the quiet power of narrative. Israel has not only defined its own enemies, it has helped define the enemies of others. By successfully conflating criticism of the Israeli state with anti-Semitism, and resistance to occupation with terrorism, it has reshaped the moral and legal boundaries of dissent.

Journalists, academics, and politicians who speak out are labelled terrorist sympathisers, security threats, or anti-Semites. The result is a chilling effect, not only on speech, but on policy. Western governments tread carefully, fearful of offending a state that has turned the label "terrorism" into a diplomatic weapon.

This strategy also affects international institutions. At the United Nations, Israel's actions are often shielded by American vetoes. Investigations into alleged war crimes are dismissed as biased or illegitimate. The International Criminal Court, mandated to act without fear or favour, has been publicly attacked for daring to even consider probes into Israeli conduct in the Occupied Territories.

The ultimate consequence of this influence is that the term "terrorist" becomes a tool of power rather than a reflection of principle. It is not applied consistently or according to law, it is wielded by those who can shape the narrative.

Israel is not unique in abusing language for political ends, but it is uniquely successful. Its model, of conflating all opposition with terrorism, framing state violence as defence, and turning moral criticism into a security risk, has been exported and adopted by others. Authoritarian regimes from Hungary to India have copied its playbook. The global war on terror, already murky, has become even more opaque.

When one country is allowed to define terrorism in its own image, and when that definition is unquestioningly adopted by powerful allies, the result is not security. It is silence. It is impunity. And it is the slow erosion of a universal moral code that was supposed to hold all actors accountable.

## Section 8: - The Export Model – How Israel's Tactics Have Been Adopted Globally

When Israel reframes its military actions as counterterrorism and casts any resistance as terrorism, it does more than silence dissent at home. It exports a model, one that has been eagerly adopted by governments around the world seeking to justify their own repression. In the post-9/11 global landscape, the Israeli playbook, merging national security with moral exceptionalism, has proven irresistible.

India under Narendra Modi has applied similar tactics in Kashmir. By branding all dissenting voices, from separatist political parties to student activists, as terrorists, the Indian state has neutralised resistance while securing international legitimacy under the guise of "fighting Islamist extremism." In the process, basic civil rights have been trampled: journalists jailed, internet access cut, and curfews imposed. Indian security forces often refer to their strategy in Kashmir as their own "Iron Dome," a telling linguistic echo of Israel's missile defence system, symbolising both technological superiority and moral justification.

In Hungary, Viktor Orbán has described asylum seekers as part of a "terrorist invasion," merging anti-immigration rhetoric with the language of counterterrorism. His administration has criminalised NGOs that assist migrants and used surveillance powers once reserved for genuine security threats against journalists and opposition figures.

Egypt's President Abdel Fattah el-Sisi has relied heavily on anti-terror laws to quash dissent. Peaceful demonstrators, LGBTQ+ citizens, and members of the Muslim Brotherhood have all been targeted under sweeping counterterrorism decrees. In justifying these moves, the Egyptian government often invokes the threat of "foreign-influenced terrorism" destabilising the region, a justification that echoes Israeli narratives about Hamas or Hezbollah.

Russia's Vladimir Putin, long adept at weaponising the language of security, has categorised critics of the war in Ukraine as extremists or foreign agents. The Russian state has banned organisations, censored protests, and jailed opposition leaders by labelling them "terrorists." Like Israel, the Russian state merges its military adventurism with a moral narrative, defence of national identity and stability.

China, too, has cited terrorism as justification for its mass internment of Uyghur Muslims in Xinjiang. In a 2019 government white paper, Beijing described its crackdown as a "counterterrorism and de-radicalisation measure," using Israel's long war against Hamas as one example of how other nations "effectively fight terrorism." In reality, the Chinese government's actions include forced labour, cultural erasure, and widespread surveillance, none of which are aimed at stopping real terror, but rather at cementing state control.

The United Kingdom has gradually slid into this export model as well. While the UK was once cautious about conflating protest with terrorism, recent years have seen a dangerous shift. Groups like Palestine Action and climate campaigners from Extinction Rebellion or Just Stop Oil have been monitored by counterterrorism units. Legislation such as the Public Order Act 2023 has created a legal grey zone where peaceful civil disobedience can be treated as a national security threat.

The defining feature of the exported model is its elasticity. Governments no longer need clear evidence of violence or credible threats, they only need to frame their opponents as enemies of the state, then wrap their repression in the language of counterterrorism. The vaguer the definition, the greater the power.

Israel's decades-long experience offers a blueprint. It has shown how to operate with impunity while retaining Western support. It has demonstrated how to silence critics by accusing them of anti-Semitism. It has taught the world how to militarise victimhood and convert it into permanent exceptionalism.

It is no coincidence that the technologies of surveillance, crowd control, and predictive policing developed by Israel have become key exports. Israeli security companies, often staffed by former military intelligence officers, provide training and hardware to police forces in the US, Brazil, India, and the Philippines. These "solutions" are not neutral, they carry with them the ideologies of their creators. When an American police force uses an Israeli crowd-control method, it is not just adopting a tactic, it is importing a worldview, one that sees protest as threat and equates security with domination.

This global export of Israel's model has led to a quiet convergence. Democracies and authoritarian regimes alike now share a vocabulary: "terror threat," "public order," "foreign influence," "national security." Behind these phrases lie sweeping powers, mass surveillance, and the suppression of dissent.

Because Israel enjoys unshakeable support from many Western allies, its model gains an aura of legitimacy. Its tactics are not seen as authoritarian overreach, but as pragmatism. Its vocabulary becomes the grammar of global security. Even critics of other regimes often hesitate to criticise Israel's influence, fearful of being branded anti-Semitic or naïve to the "complexities" of the Middle East.

The outcome is clear. As one state defines terrorism in ways that serve its own interests, others follow, adopting the definition, justifying repression, and muting opposition. What begins as a national security doctrine becomes a global template for silencing the powerless and protecting the powerful.

The label that kills is no longer confined to one region. It has gone global.

## Section 9: - When the Accused Are the Innocent – The Collapse of Due Process

Once a state labels someone a terrorist, everything changes. The presumption of innocence, once a sacred pillar of democratic jurisprudence, begins to dissolve. Suddenly, it is not what you did, but what they say you might do, or what you believe, or who you know. Guilt is no longer something proven in a court of law, but something declared in a press conference, legitimised by a security briefing, or whispered into the media by an anonymous government source.

This collapse of due process is one of the most chilling consequences of modern terrorism laws. It allows the state to reverse centuries of legal progress and democratic safeguards, often without public outcry, because "terrorism" justifies anything.

Take the United States. After 9/11, the USA PATRIOT Act granted sweeping powers to law enforcement, including the indefinite detention of non-citizens suspected of terrorism. Not convicted, suspected. Guantánamo Bay became the most notorious symbol of this collapse. Hundreds of men were held for years without charge or trial. Some were teenagers when captured, many were tortured, and the majority were eventually released without ever facing a court. As one former detainee, Mohamedou Ould Slahi, wrote in his memoir *Guantánamo Diary*: "They always told me, 'We know you're innocent, but we're never letting you go.'"

That phrase, "we know you're innocent," is not an aberration. It is the logical end point of a system that treats accusations of terrorism as tantamount to proof.

In the UK, Terrorism Prevention and Investigation Measures (TPIMs) allow the Home Secretary to impose severe restrictions—electronic tagging, travel bans, and forced relocation—on individuals without any criminal conviction. Secret intelligence can be used in court without the accused ever seeing it. In other words, people are punished without trial and without ever knowing the full case against them.

One such case involved a British man, known only as "CD," who was subjected to a TPIM for over two years, unable to challenge the full evidence against him. Eventually, the courts ruled that the evidence did not justify the order, but by then, years of his life had been upended. His movements were tracked, his relationships monitored, his freedom reduced to the length of an electronic leash.

This is what happens when due process collapses. Freedom becomes a privilege, not a right. The law becomes a performance, not a protection.

It gets worse when race or religion enters the equation. In France, the 2015 state of emergency following the Paris attacks led to thousands of warrantless raids, many targeting Muslims and North Africans. Human rights groups later found that only a handful resulted in charges. One Muslim family described their home being stormed by police in the middle of the night, their children traumatised, their neighbours whispering, their jobs lost. No weapons, no charges, no evidence, just suspicion and the stain of it forever.

In India, the draconian Unlawful Activities (Prevention) Act (UAPA) has been used to jail journalists, academics, and civil society activists. The act permits individuals to be detained for up to 180 days without a formal charge. In practice, it means people can be held for years based solely on the government's assertion that they pose a threat.

One such detainee was Stan Swamy, an 84-year-old Jesuit priest and tribal rights activist. He was arrested under UAPA in 2020 and denied proper medical treatment while in custody. He died in jail before his trial began. The charge? Alleged links to Maoist groups, based on documents many now believe were planted on his device using spyware. The state accused him, and that was enough.

The trend is international. From Turkey to Thailand, from the Philippines to Poland, governments are learning that once terrorism laws are passed, they can be weaponised, not only against terrorists, but against protestors, journalists, academics, and minorities.

The very idea of justice is transformed. Secret courts, anonymous witnesses, indefinite detention, and special police powers become standard. All the while, the public is told it is necessary, for their safety, for their freedom, for their children.

In this new landscape, innocence becomes irrelevant. What matters is the narrative. If you are labelled a terrorist, you are treated like one, no matter what the truth is.

And if you are innocent, then you are just collateral damage in a war that long ago stopped caring about facts.

## Section 10: - Domestic Extremism – When Dissent Becomes a Threat

There was a time when protesting government policies was considered a healthy feature of democracy. A sign of civic engagement. A hallmark of a free society. But in recent years, this has shifted dramatically. Peaceful protest is now frequently branded as "domestic extremism" and, in some cases, even as "terrorism." The effect is to criminalise dissent, to redraw the boundary between citizen and enemy, not by action, but by attitude.

The term "domestic extremism" is deliberately vague. It is not tied to violence. It does not require plans for a crime. It simply refers to individuals or groups whose beliefs or actions pose a perceived "threat to public order" or "national stability." In the UK, the definition used by the National Police Chiefs' Council includes those who "demonstrate a grievance or belief" that "justifies breaking the law in pursuit of a political or social cause."

That is it. Not bombs. Not terror plots. Just beliefs and the willingness to act on them through civil disobedience.

This has led to the surveillance and harassment of campaigners, academics, and climate activists under the same frameworks once reserved for violent extremists. In one instance, peaceful members of the environmental movement Extinction Rebellion were classified in police guidance alongside neo-Nazi groups and jihadi networks. Teachers were told to report students sympathetic to XR. It was only after public outcry that the classification was revised, but the message had been sent.

In the United States, the Department of Homeland Security has steadily expanded its definition of terrorism to include threats posed by so-called "anti-government" individuals. In practice, this has included Black Lives Matter protesters, pipeline resisters, and whistleblowers. In 2020, President Trump called for Antifa to be designated a terrorist organisation, despite it not being an organisation at all, but a loose, decentralised movement opposing fascism.

Compare that to how actual domestic terror threats, such as the white supremacist who bombed the Oklahoma City Federal Building or the dozens of militia groups armed to the teeth across rural America, are often treated. They are seen as troubled individuals or "lone wolves," rather than part of a broader threat. Rarely does their ideology trigger the same institutional scrutiny or panic.

In France, the Yellow Vests movement, sparked by fuel tax hikes, was met with such aggressive policing and classification as extremist that the UN warned of disproportionate force and unlawful suppression of protest. Thousands were arrested, many injured. The protest was about inequality. The response was about silencing anger.

Israel has taken this strategy to its logical conclusion. Palestinians protesting occupation, land seizures, or home demolitions are routinely described as "terrorists" before they ever throw a stone or raise a flag. Entire generations of Palestinian youth grow up being watched, interrogated, and sometimes arrested for political speech or social media posts. Even in the United States and Europe, pro-Palestine advocacy groups have found themselves under surveillance, banned from campuses, or blacklisted by financial institutions.

One especially striking case is that of the activist group Palestine Action in the UK. Their tactics, spray-painting arms company buildings or locking themselves to gates, are disruptive but non-violent. Still, the group has been branded a domestic threat, and its members face terrorism-related charges. Meanwhile, paramilitary-linked marches by proscribed loyalist groups like the UDA in Belfast have been policed peacefully, even respectfully. No mass arrests, no pre-dawn raids.

The inconsistency is glaring. Some forms of disruption are labelled extremism. Others are deemed "community events." The dividing line is not violence but politics.

The irony is that many of these activists, climate campaigners, anti-racists, and anti-war demonstrators, are trying to prevent the very violence that governments claim to oppose. They are sounding alarms about injustice, inequality, and destruction. And for this, they are being surveilled, marginalised, and sometimes imprisoned.

What is emerging is not a legal system based on the severity of an action, but one rooted in loyalty. Are you for the state or against it? Do your views challenge the dominant ideology? Are your protests inconvenient?

If the answer is yes, you may be branded a threat. Not because you are violent, but because you are right.

## Section 11: - A Global Network of Suppression – How States Learn from Each Other

The global spread of counter-terrorism laws and domestic extremism frameworks has not happened in a vacuum. It is not merely a case of parallel evolution, where governments independently arrive at the same conclusions. Rather, it is a coordinated, deliberate process built through international cooperation, security alliances, and transnational intelligence-sharing networks.

Terrorism, like capital, is now globalised. But so too is the architecture of repression.

From London to Tel Aviv, from Washington to New Delhi, a growing number of governments are learning from one another, not just how to combat legitimate threats but how to frame dissent as danger. Techniques, legal frameworks, and technologies are exported across borders. So are narratives.

The Israeli government, for instance, has long portrayed any Palestinian resistance, armed or unarmed, as terrorism. This framing has been adopted wholesale by sympathetic Western governments, especially the United States, which provides Israel with billions in military aid and routinely echoes its rhetoric. But it does not stop there. Countries like India have invoked Israel's model in Kashmir. China has used "anti-terror" arguments to justify surveillance and re-education of Uyghur Muslims. Egypt, the UAE, and Saudi Arabia have adopted counter-terrorism laws that criminalise political opposition entirely.

Britain, for its part, has become a hub for exporting surveillance techniques and protest control measures. The Prevent strategy, originally devised to counter radical Islamic terrorism, has been adapted to monitor everything from leftist student groups to climate activism. Many of the UK's tactics have been shared through the Five Eyes intelligence alliance (UK, US, Canada, Australia, New Zealand), a powerful surveillance consortium with deep influence on global security norms.

The European Union, too, has drifted toward broader definitions of extremism. Laws initially designed to tackle foreign fighters returning from Syria are now being applied to environmental activists, anti-vaccine protesters, and migrant solidarity groups. The lines between security, ideology, and inconvenience are blurring fast.

One of the most consequential examples of this trend is France's 2021 law "to reinforce respect for the principles of the Republic." Ostensibly designed to counter Islamist extremism, it imposed sweeping restrictions on civil society, tightened surveillance, and gave the state broad powers to dissolve organisations deemed a threat to "republican values." But who defines those values? And how long before the same law is turned against labour unions, protest groups, or political opponents?

Similarly, in Australia, terrorism laws have been used to detain citizens without charge, restrict movement, and even remove citizenship. In Canada, authorities invoked emergency powers to freeze the bank accounts of participants in the 2022 "Freedom Convoy" protests. These were controversial protests, but the precedent of financial weaponisation against protest was a significant escalation.

It is in this environment that organisations like Palestine Action find themselves surveilled and prosecuted. The charge is never violence—there often is none. The crime is disobedience. The crime is making people uncomfortable. And increasingly, governments are working together to ensure those who disrupt the status quo are silenced across borders.

Israel, in particular, has become a major exporter of counterinsurgency techniques. Its military, intelligence services, and private tech firms routinely collaborate with foreign governments, offering training in surveillance, crowd control, and urban warfare. These are not just tools for fighting terrorism, they are tools for managing populations.

The infamous NSO Group, for example, developed Pegasus spyware, capable of turning phones into silent surveillance devices. It has been sold to governments around the world, some of whom have used it to target journalists, lawyers, opposition leaders, and human rights activists. Victims include Jamal Khashoggi's associates, Catalan independence leaders in Spain, and critics of the Modi government in India. Israel has denied direct involvement, but the state's defence ministry licenses every export. This is not accidental. It is strategy.

Even more concerning is the normalisation of these tactics. When democracies adopt authoritarian methods, mass surveillance, pre-emptive arrests, and internet blackouts, they legitimise them. And when they collaborate with actual authoritarian regimes in doing so, the distinction between democracy and dictatorship begins to collapse.

We are now witnessing the emergence of a global security state in which governments share more with each other than they do with their citizens. Information is centralised. Dissent is decentralised. And the "war on terror" has become a portable template, rebranded for whatever domestic threat needs neutralising, be it a whistleblower, a climate striker, or a Palestinian flag.

This is not just about individual freedoms, it is about collective momentum. If every country tightens the noose simultaneously, where is the escape? Where is the sanctuary?

The danger is not just the spread of surveillance, it is the spread of permission. Once the tools exist, the temptation to use them, for political advantage, for profit, or simply for control, is almost irresistible.

As one Israeli defence contractor reportedly told a visiting foreign delegation: "We've made occupation an industry. You can too."

## Section 12: - The Future of Fear – When Security Becomes the New Ideology

In the aftermath of 9/11, the global consensus was that terrorism presented a unique and existential threat to democratic societies. Emergency powers were introduced as temporary measures. Surveillance infrastructure was rapidly expanded. Security agencies were granted unprecedented reach into the private lives of citizens, all justified by the urgency of the moment.

But the moment never ended.

What began as a reactive posture has become a governing ideology. Fear is no longer a transient emotion; it is a permanent condition. Governments across the democratic and authoritarian spectrum now operate on a shared premise: that safety justifies anything, anything at all.

The result is a world where "security" has eclipsed liberty, where pre-emptive punishment replaces due process, and where the definition of "danger" is determined not by evidence but by political expedience.

This is the future of fear.

The great irony of this moment is that even as the real threats facing the planet—climate collapse, economic instability, and resource scarcity—grow more acute, the focus of security policy remains fixated on controlling people, not solving problems. Dissenters are labelled extremists. Protest becomes sedition. And the citizen is not empowered but monitored.

We are witnessing the birth of what some analysts now call securitocracy: a form of governance in which managing perceived threats becomes the primary role of the state. Policy is no longer about progress or prosperity; it is about prevention. And in this world, terror is not an act. It is a justification.

In many ways, this ideology mirrors older authoritarian philosophies. Like communism in the Cold War or fascism in the 1930s, the security state offers a seductive promise: order through vigilance, safety through obedience. But where those systems relied on mass propaganda, the modern security state relies on algorithms, predictive policing, AI facial recognition, and silent surveillance. It is not loud. It is invisible.

And because it is invisible, it is harder to resist.

Laws designed for foreign terrorists are now applied to school climate strikers. Spyware developed to track jihadists is now found on journalists' phones. Border controls meant to deter organised crime are used to detain critics of Israel for the contents of their WhatsApp messages.

In the name of counter-terrorism, we have entered a world where:

• A 91-year-old nun protesting arms shipments can be arrested for "terrorist disruption."

• Students chanting against genocide are investigated under the Prevent duty.

• Civil society organisations are defunded for failing to demonstrate ideological purity.

And what makes this different from earlier forms of repression is not just its scope, but its respectability. The language is legal. The procedures are followed. The bureaucracy is meticulous. The tyranny is paper-thin, yet legally binding.

This is not the terror of tanks and torture. It is the terror of silent compliance.

If left unchecked, securitocracy risks becoming the new global default. Politicians will no longer need to argue for policies; they will merely need to demonstrate a risk. Opposing views will no longer be debated; they will be neutralised. And citizenship itself will become conditional, dependent on background checks, digital records, and ideological conformity.

The future of fear is one where we cease to be citizens and become subjects of surveillance. And it will not come with a bang. It will come with a court order, a software update, a briefing note, a new clause in a terrorism bill that nobody reads, until it is used against them.

If the 20th century was about the struggle between freedom and tyranny, the 21st may well be about the struggle between freedom and safety, or rather, the illusion of safety.

As we have seen again and again, fear does not make us safer. It just makes us smaller.

## Section 13: - Israel's Shadow – Exporting a Model of Permanent Security

In the global evolution of counterterrorism, no state has exerted more subtle yet far-reaching influence than Israel. Not because of its size or military might alone, but because it has redefined what "security" means and exported that definition to the world.

Israel has pioneered a model of governance rooted in permanent conflict. Since its founding, the state has framed its existence as under siege, a small democracy surrounded by hostile forces, forever fighting for survival. From this position, it has normalised a series of practices that were once considered temporary emergency responses: mass surveillance, indefinite detention, military courts for civilians, collective punishment and targeted assassinations.

What makes this model so potent is that it has been packaged as rational, efficient and high-tech. It has become the blueprint for managing unrest, protest and political opposition, not only in the West Bank and Gaza, but around the world.

And other governments have taken notice.

Israeli technology, both hardware and software, has become the backbone of border walls, biometric systems, predictive policing tools and protest-monitoring algorithms from India to Brazil, from Hungary to the United States. The spyware Pegasus, developed by Israel's NSO Group, was found on the phones of journalists, human rights activists and opposition leaders in over forty countries.

But it is not just the tools. It is the doctrine.

Israel's approach has helped recast the political landscape, in which the state claims the right to use overwhelming force not only in self-defence but in anticipation of threat. Civilian areas become legitimate targets if a militant is suspected nearby. Children throwing stones become existential risks. Hospitals can be bombed if it is claimed that a tunnel lies beneath.

As one former Israeli official remarked bluntly during a panel discussion: "In the war on terror, we cannot afford morality." That ethic, or lack of it, has travelled far.

The Hannibal Directive, the now-notorious military protocol that allowed Israeli forces to fire on vehicles or buildings suspected of containing captured soldiers, even at the risk of killing them, was originally a classified operational policy. It resurfaced in the context of 7 October 2023, when a significant number of Israeli deaths may have been caused by their own forces in line with this doctrine. Yet even this has been folded into the global security playbook, where collateral damage is reframed as unfortunate but acceptable, provided it is inflicted by a state.

What Israel exports, then, is not only equipment. It is permission. A licence to conflate dissent with danger, to blur the lines between law enforcement and war, and to suspend morality in the name of national interest.

As the war in Gaza intensified following 7 October, and Israel's campaign left over 65,000 Palestinians dead, including thousands of children, governments across Europe and North America not only stood by, they absorbed Israel's narrative wholesale. "Israel has the right to defend itself" became the reflexive mantra, even as schools, hospitals and refugee camps were bombed.

Criticism of these actions, meanwhile, was met with silence or criminalisation. In Germany, pro-Palestinian rallies were banned under the pretext of public order. In France, slogans supporting Gaza were deemed threats to national unity. In Britain, people waving Palestinian flags were reported under the Prevent duty.

This is the shadow Israel casts, not only on the Middle East but across the democratic world. A model in which the legitimacy of the state is presumed absolute, and any resistance, no matter how peaceful, is rendered suspect.

It is a model increasingly attractive to governments grappling with their own domestic crises. In an age of populism, rising inequality, mass protest and climate disruption, Israel's example offers a toolkit for managing dissent with precision, aggression and plausible deniability.

In this sense, the world has not merely stood by as Gaza burned. It has studied it, learned from it and adapted its logic to domestic conditions. In doing so, it has helped transform counterterrorism into counter-citizenship.

If the global security state now treats all protest as a precursor to terrorism, Israel's influence cannot be ignored. It has helped rewire the moral compass of democratic societies, replacing the presumption of innocence with a presumption of hostility, particularly when that hostility comes from the wrong race, the wrong faith or the wrong cause.

What begins in Gaza rarely ends there.

## Section 14: - The Blurring of Borders – From Enemy Combatants to Political Dissidents

In the shifting theatre of twenty-first-century power, the line between enemy and dissenter has all but disappeared. Once, the distinction between a foreign combatant and a domestic critic was foundational to liberal democracy. Today, it is a blur, erased by vague terror laws, aggressive policing and the globalisation of state paranoia.

Governments now increasingly treat domestic dissent as a matter of national security. Protesters are rebranded as extremists. Journalists become "information terrorists." Whistleblowers are charged under espionage laws. As the war on terror metastasised from foreign battlefields to home soil, it carried with it a chilling message: opposition equals threat.

Nowhere is this more evident than in the treatment of climate activists, Palestine solidarity campaigners and Indigenous rights defenders. These groups are rarely armed, rarely violent, but they challenge state and corporate interests. In the modern security framework, that is enough.

Consider the UK's growing use of terrorism legislation to surveil or detain peaceful activists. Under the Police, Crime, Sentencing and Courts Act, disruptive protest tactics such as blocking roads or public buildings can now carry heavy sentences. Yet it is the logic behind such moves that is more dangerous than the sentences themselves: the idea that disturbing public order is, in itself, a form of terror.

This is not incidental. It is a structural shift. Just as the "war on drugs" in the 1980s was used to criminalise Black communities in the United States, the war on terror is now being repurposed to manage political unrest in democracies. A tool of foreign policy has become an instrument of domestic control.

In France, anti-government protesters have been labelled "eco-terrorists." In India, farmers demonstrating against land reforms were branded anti-national and subjected to digital surveillance. In Canada, Indigenous pipeline protesters were monitored using counter-terror units and placed on no-fly lists.

In Palestine solidarity campaigns across Europe and North America, peaceful protestors find themselves arrested, smeared or placed under surveillance, despite never advocating violence.

This new security paradigm does not merely suppress dissent. It redefines who gets to dissent. The power to label someone a threat lies entirely with the state. Once that label is applied, whether "extremist," "sympathiser" or "agitator," the normal protections of democracy begin to melt away.

Legal safeguards are circumvented in the name of national security. Free speech is conditioned on whether the speech challenges the status quo. Peaceful assembly is permitted only if it avoids inconvenience. The public, bombarded with fear-based narratives, is taught to cheer these measures as necessary rather than dangerous.

In the United States, the Department of Homeland Security now works closely with local police to monitor "radicalising behaviours." This includes attending certain events, associating with activists or using specific phrases online. It is not a conspiracy. It is policy.

Technology accelerates the blurring. Predictive policing algorithms, often trained on biased data, reinforce pre-existing prejudices. Social media monitoring tools flag keywords and hashtags associated with "threat groups." Protest planning is treated like insurgency. Surveillance becomes pre-emptive, and guilt is inferred from proximity.

All of it is justified by invoking "public safety" and "prevention of terrorism," terms that, without a universal definition of terrorism, can be stretched to cover almost anything.

The danger here is not hypothetical. It is cumulative. It chips away at civil liberties one act at a time, until the only people allowed to dissent are those the state deems harmless. Dissent becomes a licensed performance, not a democratic right.

What we are witnessing is a quiet inversion of democratic principles. The citizen is no longer presumed to be acting in good faith. The burden of proof shifts. You are not free until proven guilty. You are guilty until the state chooses not to act.

The war on terror was supposed to be fought to protect freedom. Instead, it has created a system in which the freedom to protest, to speak and to expose abuse has become conditional.

And it is happening in full view.

As rights groups warn of chilling effects on activism, as journalists are detained for covering protests and as courts begin to interpret law through a national security lens, the transformation of liberal democracy into a surveillance state creeps forward.

Israel's influence is not alone in this shift, but it is illustrative. A country where the occupation of territory has required the permanent suppression of another people cannot avoid exporting that logic when it exports its tools, tactics and justifications.

The global consequence is an international norm in which it is not what you do, but what you oppose, that determines your status in the eyes of the state.

In such a world, the real threat to security is not the terrorist with a bomb. It is the dissenter with a banner. Increasingly, the state treats both the same.

## Section 15: - The Collapse of Consent – Democracy Under Siege

In every democracy, there exists a fragile, often unspoken contract between the governed and those who govern. At its core is the idea of consent, consent to be ruled, to be taxed, to abide by laws and to trust in institutions. This consent is not permanent. It is constantly renewed through elections, public discourse and the belief that systems can be held accountable. When that belief falters, when trust erodes and dissent is criminalised, the contract begins to tear. What fills the void is something far more dangerous: coercion in the place of consensus, and fear in the place of freedom.

The war on terror has helped accelerate that shift.

What began as an exceptional response to an exceptional threat, al-Qaeda, 9/11 and suicide bombings, has become a permanent architecture of suspicion. Governments across the democratic world have retooled the very meaning of governance. Where once legitimacy rested on representation and transparency, it now often rests on control and the perception of strength.

This shift can be seen not just in laws, but in the tone of leadership. In the language of power.

The politician who once promised hope now invokes danger. The citizen once seen as a participant is recast as a potential threat. From the United States to the United Kingdom, from India to Israel, the consent of the governed is replaced by a performance of security, where fear justifies surveillance and dissent is managed, not listened to.

The collapse of consent does not happen with a bang. It happens with bureaucratic efficiency.

Laws are passed quietly. Protests are restricted by new conditions. Arrests are made under the broad shadow of "extremism." Journalists are denied access and activists find their bank accounts frozen or their travel blocked. The public, exhausted or distracted, barely notices. Yet the implications are profound.

Because without consent, democracy is just theatre.

It is not enough to hold elections. Even authoritarian regimes do that. What makes a democracy live and breathe is the mutual trust that power is exercised on behalf of the people, and that power can be challenged without fear of being labelled an enemy of the state.

When that challenge becomes suspect, when courts favour security over rights and when governments define legitimacy not by performance but by compliance, we are no longer in a democracy. We are in a managed society. A controlled one. A fragile one.

In this new world, consent is not given. It is extracted.

The chilling effect on civic life is unmistakable. People self-censor. Civil society groups adopt legal disclaimers and "apolitical" language. Campaigns are waged in whispers. Teachers fear speaking truth in classrooms. Councillors fear tweeting solidarity with the oppressed. Everything becomes performative, cautious, indirect.

Into that vacuum comes the strongman, the nationalist, the demagogue. He promises order. He promises protection. He names enemies. He offers to carry the burden of freedom by limiting it.

It is a seductive offer.

But it is a false one.

The consequence of collapsing consent is not greater security. It is permanent instability. When people are denied the means to express dissent peacefully, they will find other ways. History is replete with regimes that believed control equalled peace, only to discover that silence is not compliance, it is pressure building.

This chapter of history is being written now. It demands vigilance.

Once the democratic contract is broken, restoring it is far harder than preserving it. If we continue to conflate protest with terror, criticism with extremism and journalism with subversion, then we will find ourselves governed not by consent, but by coercion dressed as patriotism.

It is not too late to stop that slide. But it requires courage: the courage to defend the inconvenient, the unpopular and the dissenting. The courage to say that true security lies not in silencing voices, but in hearing them.

Because a democracy that cannot tolerate dissent has already ceased to be one.

## Section 16: - From Pre-Crime to Pre-Guilt – The Future of Repression

In the world being shaped by post 9/11 counterterrorism doctrine and twenty first century authoritarian creep, a dangerous evolution is underway. We are moving from punishing crimes to pre-empting them, not based on action, evidence or even intent, but on suspicion, profile and possibility. This is not science fiction. It is the logic underpinning modern counterterrorism strategies across democracies and autocracies alike. The age of pre-crime is here, and with it, pre-guilt.

In practice, this shift is visible in the growing use of Prevent style programmes in the UK and other countries, where children have been interrogated by police or referred to authorities for drawings, essays or conversations deemed "suspicious." A seven year old in London was once referred to counterterrorism authorities for saying "eco-terrorist" in a school discussion about climate change. A teenager was detained under suspicion of radicalisation for reading literature critical of colonialism. These are not isolated examples. They reflect a state mindset that sees danger not in what people do, but in what they might think.

In the United States, the concept of "radicalisation indicators" has been used to monitor and flag individuals who attend mosques, express dissent on social media or criticise United States foreign policy. Such indicators are dangerously vague and deeply racialised. Muslim communities in particular have borne the brunt of this surveillance regime, though recent years have also seen activists from Black Lives Matter, climate movements and even teachers' unions labelled as "extremists" or "domestic threats."

The problem is not simply who is being watched, but how justice is being redefined. Pre-crime policies assume guilt before any act is committed. They remove the presumption of innocence and invert it, so you are dangerous unless you can prove otherwise. The psychological burden of living under such a cloud, especially for marginalised groups, is immense. Trust erodes. Fear becomes endemic. Surveillance becomes a daily presence, not an exceptional measure.

This logic is also visible in new digital surveillance infrastructures. Algorithms now flag "anomalous behaviour." AI systems comb through facial recognition databases, shopping records, location data and online speech to determine potential threats. Yet algorithms, trained on biased data, do not eliminate prejudice. They automate it. As Edward Snowden once warned, "What is being built is the architecture of oppression."

Pre-guilt is no longer limited to the individual. Whole communities are now designated as suspect. The labelling of Palestine Action, environmental groups or Tamil diaspora organisations as extremist, despite no proven record of violence, reflects a broader strategy to criminalise dissent before it even arises. It is not about justice. It is about control.

This evolution also reveals the fragility of democratic oversight. Anti-terror laws are passed swiftly, with little public scrutiny, often under the justification of national security or the latest manufactured panic. Emergency powers become permanent. Dissenters are demonised. Politicians invoke "common sense security" while quietly building surveillance states whose reach and logic would make Orwell blush.

And it will not stop here. Predictive policing, biometric categorisation and the expansion of extrajudicial punishment are all on the horizon. What begins as a war on terror becomes a war on dissent, difference and ultimately democracy itself. The tools created to prevent violence are increasingly being used to pre-empt resistance.

The global consequence of all this is devastating. International law is being replaced by pre-emptive doctrine, and those labelled "dangerous" by the powerful are increasingly silenced without trial, without transparency and without recourse.

We began with the question: what is terrorism? Yet we now find ourselves confronting a different one.

What becomes of a society where guilt precedes action and suspicion is sufficient for punishment? The answer may be the most terrifying conclusion of all.

# CHAPTER FOURTEEN

## Section 1: - The Hollowing of a Word

"Terrorism" once carried a clear and chilling resonance. It conjured images of deliberate attacks on civilians, ideologically driven violence, and the calculated use of fear to achieve political aims. It was a label reserved for the most shocking acts, including the IRA bombing campaigns, the September 11 attacks and the Bataclan massacre. But today, the term has become elastic, malleable and, in many cases, meaningless, stretched to fit a variety of political agendas and stripped of consistent moral or legal substance. In the twenty-first century, terrorism is less about what you do and more about who you are, or who you are perceived to be.

This semantic erosion did not happen by accident. It is the result of a decades-long process in which states have deliberately blurred the boundaries of the word for strategic advantage. The "war on terror" was not just a military doctrine; it was a linguistic and legal one. It allowed governments to determine unilaterally who was a terrorist, which groups qualified as threats and which legal norms could be suspended in response. It empowered states to bypass traditional constraints on power under the guise of emergency and fear, in a process reminiscent of Carl Schmitt's warning that "sovereign is he who decides on the exception."

This power to define terrorism has produced a grotesque irony. While the term was once used to condemn acts of mass violence, it is now equally used to suppress speech, target minorities or criminalise protest. A climate activist chaining herself to a fence may now face terrorism charges, while a drone operator annihilating a village in a "suspected militant zone" faces commendation. This moral inversion is not accidental; it is a direct product of how power redefines threat.

In this climate, even innocence offers no protection. In *The Politics of Rage*, I explored how populist leaders use fear to consolidate authority, defining the enemy, stoking panic and then presenting themselves as the only solution. Terrorism plays a key role in this narrative. It creates the pretext for emergency powers, for surveillance creep and for the erosion of rights and civil liberties. It is remarkably effective because it short-circuits rational thought. Once someone is labelled a terrorist, the public demands punishment, not justice.

Nowhere is this clearer than in the double standard of its application. Israel's actions in Gaza, for instance, with tens of thousands dead, entire neighbourhoods levelled and civilian infrastructure deliberately targeted, are rarely, if ever, described as terrorism. Meanwhile, groups like Palestine Action, who commit no violent acts but deface property to protest war crimes, are rapidly prosecuted under terrorism legislation. What we are witnessing is not just hypocrisy; it is a systemic misuse of language to serve geopolitical interests.

The term "terrorism" has become so pliable that it can be used to describe a violent armed insurgency and a non-violent blockade of an arms factory. Its definitional scope now encompasses too much and yet not enough. It cannot explain why state-sponsored violence is excused, or why entire populations can be bombed, starved or surveilled without triggering the label. As I wrote in *The Rise and Fall of Zionism in the 21st Century*, the word has become a shield for some and a sword for others, determined not by moral consistency but by international alliances and propaganda.

This erosion of clarity weakens international law, undermines public trust and jeopardises real efforts to combat violence. If everything is terrorism, then nothing is. And if the label is applied only to enemies of the state, it becomes little more than a political tool, a euphemism for dissent or a justification for war.

In the next section, we will explore how this dilution of meaning has not only failed to stop terrorism but has, in some cases, actively fuelled it, by driving radicalisation, undermining legitimate protest and empowering authoritarian regimes across the globe.

## Section 2: - Fuel on the Fire – How the Misuse of "Terrorism" Creates More of It

Every time a peaceful protestor is arrested under anti-terrorism laws, a message is sent, not just to that individual but to entire communities. It says, "Dissent is dangerous. Obedience is safety." But paradoxically, this heavy-handed response does not quell discontent; it radicalises it. The overuse and misuse of terrorism legislation often serve as accelerants rather than deterrents, turning frustration into fury and grievance into ideology.

Across the globe, young people are watching their peers imprisoned for holding placards, occupying public buildings or refusing to comply with security forces. From Paris to Portland, from Tel Aviv to Tehran, state responses have been strikingly similar: surveillance, infiltration, blacklisting and detention, all justified under the vague umbrella of national security. But as history repeatedly shows, when democratic channels for protest are blocked or criminalised, underground movements flourish. When all forms of resistance are labelled terrorism, those with genuine grievances may conclude that they have nothing left to lose.

This phenomenon is not new. The British Empire's brutal suppression of independence movements in India and Kenya only strengthened the resolve of those who would later be called freedom fighters. Nelson Mandela's African National Congress (ANC) was once classified as a terrorist organisation by the United States, as was Mandela himself until 2008. Yet when peaceful channels were closed, violent resistance was seen by many as the only remaining path to liberation.

Today, that cycle continues in places like Gaza, Kashmir and even Western liberal democracies. When protestors in the UK are arrested under counter-terror laws for chanting slogans or waving Palestinian flags, the message received is not one of public safety; it is one of systemic injustice. The same applies in France, where Muslim communities feel the brunt of aggressive counter-extremism policies that criminalise speech and restrict religious expression under the guise of "republican values."

What results is a combustible mix of alienation and anger. Marginalised populations begin to see the system as inherently hostile, and the state's language of security as code for repression. Once that perception takes hold, even moderate voices struggle to make the case for peaceful engagement. Into this void step more extreme actors, offering the clarity and defiance that disillusioned youth crave.

Worse still, the state's disproportionate focus on certain groups feeds a broader narrative of injustice. Islamist groups, for instance, are scrutinised with laser intensity, while right-wing extremists, including those linked to political violence and hate crimes, often slip through the net. This discrepancy is not lost on communities already under surveillance. It breeds resentment, reinforces the belief that justice is selective and makes extremist recruitment all the easier.

Professor Jeffrey Sachs, in his broader critique of Western foreign policy, has repeatedly argued that the seeds of much of today's violence were sown by imperial arrogance and a refusal to reckon with historical crimes. "The instability we see," Sachs once told the UN, "is the harvest of empire." When states not only fail to acknowledge their role in creating these grievances but also weaponise language to silence them, they create the very threats they claim to fight.

By labelling all forms of protest as terrorism, the state undermines its own legitimacy. It turns law enforcement into a political tool and delegitimises genuine efforts to counter real threats. More tragically, it drowns out the voices of victims, those caught between the twin abuses of extremist violence and state repression. These are the people who deserve our protection, yet their suffering is often ignored, their words discredited simply because they are inconvenient to the dominant narrative.

And so, the cycle deepens. Protest becomes repression, repression breeds anger, anger fuels resistance and all of it is recast in the simplistic binary of terrorist versus state. It is a cycle we must break, and that begins with reclaiming the word "terrorism" from those who have used it not to protect lives but to entrench power.

## Section 3: - The War on Terror's Legacy – A Generation Shaped by Fear

Two decades on from the fall of the Twin Towers, the children born in the shadow of that event have grown up in a world where "terror" is not only a media staple but a daily political justification. They have never known a society not at war with an idea, a shapeless and evolving threat that justifies everything from surveillance and drone strikes to airport pat-downs and pre-crime laws. This generation, millennials and Gen Z alike, has been shaped not by the threat of terrorism itself but by the political response to it. That response has left a deep generational scar.

The "War on Terror" was sold to the public as a necessary evil, a battle to preserve freedom even if it required temporarily restricting it. But as the years passed, those temporary measures ossified into permanent structures. The Patriot Act never truly expired. Guantanamo Bay still has not closed. Black sites, extraordinary renditions, and indefinite detention without trial became not the dark exception but the norm. And young people watched.

They watched as whistleblowers like Edward Snowden were exiled and as Julian Assange was hunted and imprisoned, not for committing violence but for revealing it. They saw Muslim communities targeted disproportionately by law enforcement. They witnessed anti-terror laws creeping into every corner of civil life, used against environmentalists, student activists, and journalists. The message they absorbed was not one of safety but of suspicion. Trust in institutions began to erode. Skepticism toward the state became the default, not the exception.

Surveillance, once the domain of dystopian fiction, became a daily reality. Cameras on every street corner. Algorithms combing through social media. Facial recognition software rolled out without consent. In schools, children were referred to counter-terrorism programmes for writing about Palestine or asking about Islam. In the workplace, employees were monitored, their private opinions potentially grounds for discipline. This was not Orwell's *1984*. This was post-9/11 liberal democracy. And it was all justified under the rubric of security.

But the long-term legacy is not security. It is cynicism. A whole generation has grown up internalising the idea that the state does not act in their interest but in its own. That the line between governance and control is thinner than ever. That speaking out can make you a suspect. In many cases, this has led to disengagement. Why vote if the system is rigged? Why protest if you will be labelled a threat? Why believe in democracy if the democratic state behaves like an authoritarian one?

We are now witnessing the consequences. Young people are turning away from legacy politics, embracing either radical alternatives or apathy. Many no longer believe in the benevolence of the West, particularly when they see Gaza bombed with impunity or Yemen starved in silence. The credibility gap between the rhetoric of freedom and the reality of repression has widened so much that it threatens the social contract itself.

And yet, politicians and policymakers remain fixated on terror as a unifying threat. They double down on laws that criminalise dissent and on policies that profile and persecute, convinced that they are protecting their societies. In truth, they are corroding the foundations of civic trust. They are telling a generation, in word and deed, that fear is the defining feature of modern citizenship.

The ultimate irony is that the "War on Terror" has not made us safer. It has made us more fearful, more divided, and more vulnerable to extremism from all sides. It has trained us to see enemies everywhere, to doubt each other, and to accept the unacceptable in the name of security. In doing so, it has shaped a generation that questions whether the greatest threat to their freedom comes not from a distant cave in Afghanistan but from the governments that claim to defend it.

## Section 4: - The Final Victim – Democracy Itself

Democracy, once heralded as the triumph of the modern world, is quietly bleeding out under the weight of the very war waged in its name. While flags still fly, elections are still held, and parliaments still convene, the substance of democracy, its freedoms, its checks and balances, and its foundational trust between citizen and state, has been hollowed out. Not with tanks on the streets or coups in the night, but with legal clauses, emergency powers, and the slow, insidious creep of a fear that has become institutionalised.

The post-9/11 era gave rise to an architecture of control that now operates independently of crisis. What were once extraordinary powers granted in moments of national trauma have become the default tools of governance. Anti-terrorism legislation, supposedly designed to prevent violence, has become a Swiss Army knife for suppressing dissent. Peaceful protest can be labelled extremist.

Organising online can be treated as a threat. Political movements, even if entirely non-violent, are now scrutinised through the lens of radicalisation. The bar for being branded a national security risk is lower than ever and far more subjective.

This is not theoretical. It is playing out in real time. In the UK, the Police, Crime, Sentencing and Courts Act has empowered authorities to criminalise peaceful protest based on noise levels. In France, President Macron's government has pushed through sweeping anti-separatism laws under the guise of countering Islamist extremism, laws that critics argue disproportionately target Muslim communities. In India, Prime Minister Modi has used counter-terror laws to imprison dissenters, journalists, and students. In the United States, the Capitol riot of 6 January 2021 provided the pretext for expanding surveillance and re-energising the domestic terror apparatus, ironically under a president who had previously cheered on state violence.

Perhaps nowhere is the erosion of democracy more visible than in Israel, a state that presents itself as a liberal democracy but behaves increasingly like an ethno-nationalist security state. The bombardment of Gaza, the silencing of domestic critics, and the outlawing of Palestinian organisations are all justified through the same invocation of security. Yet this security has come at the expense of pluralism, accountability, and human rights. It has turned democracy into a mask for permanent war. It is no coincidence that many Western democracies now echo these justifications in their own internal repression.

We must ask ourselves what kind of democracy survives if it requires mass surveillance to function. If it sees its own people as potential threats. If it outlaws solidarity, punishes journalism, and criminalises opposition. At what point does the democratic façade become a cover for something altogether more sinister?

The final victim of the War on Terror may not be a nation or a community. It may be the very idea of democracy itself. A democracy that fears its own citizens cannot claim to be free. A democracy that equates criticism with treason cannot call itself open. A democracy that borrows the tools of authoritarianism and forgets to return them cannot survive.

This is the paradox of our age. The war that was launched to defend democracy has, in the end, made democracy more fragile than at any point in recent history. In fighting the spectre of terrorism, we have given birth to something more enduring, more invasive, and more corrosive. Not terror itself but a state of permanent suspicion, unaccountable power, and institutionalised fear.

The greatest threat to our democracy may no longer come from bombs or guns but from the laws, systems, and narratives we have built to prevent them.

## Section 5: - What Comes Next?

If the war on terror has hollowed out our democracies, redefined dissent as danger, and granted unprecedented powers to the state, then what comes next? What kind of world are we walking into, or sleepwalking through, as we redefine terrorism not by the nature of the act but by the identity of the actor?

The answer may lie in two directions: the continuation of authoritarian drift, or a collective awakening. And the choice, though narrowing, still exists.

In one version of the future, the boundaries between surveillance and life blur entirely. Facial recognition becomes routine, not just at borders or in airports, but in high streets, sports events, and classrooms. AI-driven prediction tools, already tested in policing, extend into healthcare, education, and welfare under the guise of "risk management." Journalists tread carefully, knowing whistleblowers are hunted. Protestors gather in shrinking numbers, deterred not by water cannons but by arrest records that follow them into every job interview.

Political activism becomes a liability. People learn to censor themselves in the quiet corners of their lives, at dinner tables, in WhatsApp groups, and on job applications, simply to avoid drawing the wrong kind of attention. Dissent becomes not dangerous, but rare. And all of this, crucially, will be carried out not by dictators, but by democratically elected leaders in "free" societies.

In this world, the very language of freedom becomes a camouflage. Authoritarianism does not arrive with a fist raised; it arrives with a smile, a policy paper, a counter-extremism strategy, a patriotism test. The machinery of democracy remains, but its spirit is gone. As the Israeli security model is exported around the globe, surveillance-heavy, militarised, and suspicious of dissent, the global norm becomes one of control. And all of it is justified, still, in the name of fighting "terror."

But there is another path.

In this version, the public begins to reckon with the price we have paid. Citizens see that anti-terror laws have become tools of domestic suppression. That surveillance is not about safety but about power. That the greatest violence is sometimes committed by those wearing the uniform of the state. That Palestinians, Afghans, Iraqis, and others were not footnotes in our war on terror; they were the victims. That Julian Assange, Edward Snowden, and countless unnamed whistleblowers were not traitors; they were prophets. That every protestor arrested for holding a banner, every activist branded an extremist, was not a threat, but a warning.

In this future, we dismantle what we built in fear. We repeal the most repressive laws. We rebuild journalism as a public good. We recognise that terrorism cannot be fought by redefining it to suit our interests. That extremism is not stopped by silencing voices, but by addressing grievances. That the best defence of democracy is not more power to the state, but more rights to the people.

This future will not arrive easily. It demands courage. It demands that we confront our own complicity. That we look not only at the Trumps, Netanyahus, and Putins of the world, but at ourselves: our silence, our fear, our surrender to comfort. It demands we ask uncomfortable questions. Why do we fear some violence more than others? Why do some lives matter more? Why do we call some acts terrorism, and others collateral damage?

Ultimately, "what comes next" is not a question for governments alone. It is a question for each of us. What will we tolerate? What will we resist? What kind of world will we defend?

We began this century with a promise to root out terror. In the process, we have sown fear, suspicion, and authoritarianism. The next chapter depends on whether we can find the courage to call that out, and to rewrite the script.

## Section 6: - The Final Reckoning

*"The greatest trick the Devil ever pulled was convincing the world he didn't exist."* That line from *The Usual Suspects* echoes loudly in this century's greatest deception: the redefinition of terrorism. Not by clarity, but by confusion. Not by precision, but by manipulation. And not to protect people, but to control them.

As we reach the end of this journey, the reckoning is no longer just about what terrorism is. It is about what it has become, and what has been done in its name.

Terrorism today is a label wielded with surgical intent. It silences protest. It justifies war. It criminalises solidarity. It protects state violence. And yet, all the while, it cloaks itself in legitimacy. In law. In patriotism. In the illusion of consensus. It no longer needs to justify itself, because we have stopped questioning it.

That is the trick. The sleight of hand. We still see terrorism everywhere, in headlines, in policy, in public fears, but we have lost sight of its true meaning. The power of the label is not in what it reveals, but in what it obscures. It hides state terror behind security. It hides injustice behind legality. It hides racism behind risk assessment. It makes certain violence unspeakable, and other violence a daily routine.

So how do we reckon with this?

We begin by restoring meaning to the word itself. Not by accepting a single definition, but by rejecting the self-serving ones. We must insist that terrorism is not defined by uniforms, passports, or national flags. It is defined by the deliberate use of fear, violence, and intimidation against civilians, whoever commits it.

That means confronting the terror inflicted by drones, by sanctions, by siege, and by policy. It means acknowledging the terror felt by Gazan children under bombardment, by whistleblowers locked away for telling the truth, by protestors dragged from the streets for holding banners, by Indigenous communities bulldozed out of their land in the name of "development."

The reckoning also requires humility. The West cannot lead the fight against terrorism while refusing to look in the mirror. We cannot export human rights with one hand while eroding them at home with the other. We cannot lecture others about extremism while criminalising our own activists. We cannot talk about freedom if we are afraid of our own citizens speaking freely.

And perhaps most importantly, we must unlearn the conditioning that some violence is normal, excusable, or invisible. Because once we accept that premise, that some bombs are more moral than others, that some deaths are more regrettable, that some bodies matter less, then we are lost.

The path forward is not easy. It means defending free speech even when it makes us uncomfortable. It means holding allies accountable. It means protecting those who challenge power, not punishing them. It means creating a world where terrorism is named not for political convenience, but with moral consistency.

My other books, *The Politics of Rage*, *The Rise and Fall of Zionism*, and *The Pitchforks Are Coming*, each interrogated the abuses of power, the manipulation of public fear, and the erosion of truth. *Are You A Terrorist?* brings those threads together with one final warning: when a word loses its meaning, it becomes a weapon.

Terrorism has become that weapon.

This is the reckoning. And the choice, as always, is ours.

# Conclusion

In an age of surveillance, spin, and selective memory, the word "terrorism" no longer illuminates, it obscures. It has become a catch-all, a cudgel, and a cover story. Throughout this book, I have attempted to peel back the layers, from the legal distortions and political hypocrisies to the lived experiences of those targeted, silenced, or erased. The power of the label lies not in its accuracy but in its effect, to criminalise dissent, to excuse state violence, and to divide the world into "us" and "them." If we are to reclaim any moral clarity, we must confront this distortion head-on. Because in the end, the fight is not just over words, it is over who gets to define reality, who gets to speak, and who gets to be heard. That is the real battle.

That is the unfinished work.

**The Final Verdict**

In writing this book, I began with a question. A question I have asked time and time again as a writer, as a citizen, and as a witness to the unravelling of global norms: what does the word "terrorist" really mean, and who decides?

I have spent much of my 70 years watching how the label is applied, selectively, politically, often cynically. And the more I have studied, the more disturbing the pattern becomes. The word no longer describes the act. It describes the actor. It is not about what is done, it is about who does it and whether they wear a uniform or wave a flag.

We are living through an era where language itself has been weaponised. Where protest is persecution. Where journalism is espionage. Where children buried in rubble are explained away as "human shields." Where surveillance masquerades as safety, and complicity is rebranded as patriotism.

I have written other books, *The Politics of Rage*, *The Pitchforks Are Coming*, and *The Rise and Fall of Zionism in the 21st Century*, but none have felt quite so urgent as this one. Because this is not just about war, or law, or policy. This is about whether the world we are building still has a place for justice, for truth, for conscience.

The greatest danger we face today is not from those who commit acts of terror. It is from those who redefine the word until it applies to anyone who resists.

Who protests.

Who speaks out.

Who refuses to forget.

If you oppose injustice, are you a terrorist?

If you refuse silence in the face of atrocity, are you a threat?

If you demand accountability from powerful nations and their allies, do you make yourself a target?

These are not rhetorical questions. They are the warning signs of what happens when democracy erodes and fear is used as fuel. We have seen this before. We know where it leads.

And so, the final verdict is this: terrorism is no longer a term of law. It is a tool of power. A shape-shifting label, deployed not to define violence, but to defend it. And unless we reclaim the word, and with it the principles of fairness, consistency, and truth, we may all wake up one day to find that we too have been redefined.

Because in the eyes of the powerful, the greatest crime may not be violence at all.

It may simply be dissent.

# References

## Books and Academic Works:

- Chomsky, Noam. *Power and Terror: Post-9/11 Talks and Interviews*. Seven Stories Press, 2003.

- Fanon, Frantz. *The Wretched of the Earth*. Grove Press, 1963.

- Mamdani, Mahmood. *Good Muslim, Bad Muslim: America, the Cold War, and the Roots of Terror*. Pantheon Books, 2004.

- Pape, Robert A. *Dying to Win: The Strategic Logic of Suicide Terrorism*. Random House, 2005.

- Scahill, Jeremy. *Dirty Wars: The World Is a Battlefield*. Nation Books, 2013.

- Sachs, Jeffrey D. *The Price of Civilization*. Random House, 2011.

- Orwell, George. *1984*. Secker & Warburg, 1949.

## Reports and Legal Documents:

- United Nations General Assembly Resolution 57/219 (2002).

- United Nations Commission on Human Rights Resolution 2003/68.

- UN Global Counter-Terrorism Strategy (2006, updated 2021).

- Office of the High Commissioner for Human Rights, "Human Rights and Counterterrorism" Briefing Papers.

- European Court of Human Rights, judgments on extraordinary rendition and surveillance.

- US Congressional Record – Espionage Act Cases and Press Freedom.

**News and Journalism:**

- Al Jazeera. "Julian Assange: 'I Pled Guilty to Journalism.'" Strasbourg Address, July 2025.
- The Guardian. "Hannibal Directive: Israeli Forces Open Fire on Own Civilians during October 7th Attack." November 2024.
- Haaretz. "IDF Reveals Use of Hannibal Procedure on October 7." December 2024.
- BBC News. "PSNI Police and the UDA Parade: No Arrests Despite Terror Links." July 2025.
- The Intercept. "Drone Warfare and Targeted Killings: US Accountability Gap." March 2023.
- The New York Times. "Israeli Bombing in Gaza: A Timeline of Escalation." 2024–2025 coverage.
- Channel 4 Dispatches. "Children of the Rubble: Gaza's Unexploded Bombs." April 2025.

**Speeches and Testimonies:**

- Julian Assange, Address to the Parliamentary Assembly of the Council of Europe, Strasbourg, July 2025.
- Edward Snowden, Remote Testimony to the EU Parliament, 2014.
- Gideon Levy, Haaretz Columns and Interviews (2015–2025).
- Professor Jeffrey Sachs, Speech to UN Human Rights Council, March 2025.
- Merav Michaeli (Israeli Knesset), Interview on Political Incitement and Netanyahu, October 2022.

**Miscellaneous and Online Sources:**

- UN Office of Counterterrorism (UNOCT) Website: www.un.org/counterterrorism

- Amnesty International Reports on Israel and Gaza, 2023–2025.

- Human Rights Watch Country Briefs: Israel/Palestine, US, UK, Russia.

- Council of Europe, Press Freedom and Digital Surveillance Reports, 2024–2025.

This reference list combines primary sources, investigative journalism, academic material, and official documentation cited throughout the manuscript. Additional references can be appended as the final manuscript is proofread and finalised.

www.ingramcontent.com/pod-product-compliance
Lightning Source LLC
Chambersburg PA
CBHW041932260326
41914CB00010B/1274